Praise for *The Reputation Advantage*

"Reputation is built through the everyday experiences that connect brands to people's lives, and few leaders understand that better than Chris Foster. *The Reputation Advantage* offers a compelling framework for turning trust, relevance, and stakeholder confidence into enterprise value."

—**Anton Vincent,** president of Mars Snacking NA
and Global Ice Cream

"Chris Foster makes a powerful case that reputation is not a soft measure of perception but a strategic asset that shapes trust, growth, and long-term enterprise value. *The Reputation Advantage* is an essential read for leaders who understand that enduring brands are built through clarity, credibility, and consistent action."

—**Jerri DeVard,** founder and CEO of the
Black Executive CMO Alliance (BECA)

"Reputation is built where brand, corporate affairs, and business strategy meet, and Chris Foster brings that connection into sharp focus. *The Reputation Advantage* offers a clear and practical framework for leaders navigating transformation, stakeholder expectations, and the enterprise value created through trust, clarity, and relevance."

—**Leslie McGibbon,** chief corporate affairs
and brand officer at BT Group

"In *The Reputation Advantage*, Chris Foster offers a timely and thoughtful framework for understanding reputation as enterprise capital and for helping leaders build the trust, clarity, and the permission required to lead effectively."

—**Jesse Scinto,** deputy program director of the Strategic Communication program at Columbia University

"Reputation is built through the choices organizations make, the stories they tell, and the confidence they create with every stakeholder touchpoint. Chris Foster offers an insightful framework for leaders operating in complex, high-impact industries where credibility, clarity, and enterprise value are deeply connected."

—**Josh Byerly,** chief communications officer at SLB

"Chris Foster makes a compelling case that reputation is one of the most important forms of capital any modern organization can build. *The Reputation Advantage* speaks directly to leaders navigating the future of business, creativity, and culture, offering a clear framework for turning trust, relevance, and stakeholder confidence into measurable enterprise value."

—**Justin Thomas-Copeland,** CEO of the 4As

"Chris Foster's *The Reputation Advantage* is a must-read for leaders navigating global complexity. The book shows how lasting success comes from connecting dots across markets, stakeholders, and moments, and from treating reputation as a strategic system, not a reactive function."

—**Jim Margolis,** partner at GMMB

"Chris Foster reframes reputation as a form of enterprise capital that leaders must understand, build, and apply with intention. *The Reputation Advantage* offers a practical and timely framework for professionals and organizations navigating change, showing how trust, clarity, and stakeholder confidence can strengthen leadership and unlock new value."

–**Melissa Lubin,** dean of the University of Virginia School of Continuing and Professional Studies

"Chris Foster has led global brands through crises, repositioning and explaining to the world why they deserve to be recognized. In *The Reputation Advantage*, Chris lays out the approaches required to win in today's ever-changing landscape."

–**Terry Nelson,** partner at PLUS Communications

"*The Reputation Advantage* makes a clear case for what leaders increasingly know but rarely operationalize: Reputation is not a communications outcome. It is an enterprise system. Chris Foster shows how organizations can connect signals across markets, stakeholders, policy, and culture and turn that alignment into durable business advantage."

–**Robin Callif,** chief communications officer at Omnicom Public Relations

THE REPUTATION ADVANTAGE

THE REPUTATION ADVANTAGE

The Strategic Multiplier Behind Growth, Market Access, and Long-Term Value

Chris Foster

FC
FAST
COMPANY
Press

Fast Company Press
New York, New York
www.fastcompanypress.com

Distributed by Greenleaf Book Group

For ordering information or special discounts for bulk purchases, please contact Greenleaf Book Group at PO Box 91869, Austin, TX 78709, 512.891.6100.

Design and composition by Greenleaf Book Group
Cover design by Cliff Commanday

Publisher's Cataloging-in-Publication data is available.

Print ISBN: 978-1-63908-200-1

eBook ISBN: 978-1-63908-201-8

To offset the number of trees consumed in the printing of our books, Greenleaf donates a portion of the proceeds from each printing to the Arbor Day Foundation. Greenleaf Book Group has replaced over 50,000 trees since 2007.

Printed in the United States of America on acid-free paper

26 27 28 29 30 31 32 33 10 9 8 7 6 5 4 3 2 1

First Edition

CONTENTS

PART IV: THEORY AND FRAMEWORKS

ACKNOWLEDGMENTS

This book is the result of many conversations, collaborations, and shared explorations over the past several years. What began as a continuation of earlier thinking has evolved into something far more grounded, shaped by real-world application, challenge, and refinement alongside several trusted partners.

I am especially grateful to Jeanine Moss and Nicole DeMeo at Outfront Solutions. Their partnership over the past year has been instrumental in bringing many of the ideas in this book to life. Together, we have tested, challenged, and strengthened these concepts in real-world environments, and their insight, rigor, and support have meaningfully shaped the thinking captured in these pages.

My thanks also go to Mike Barlow, who served as editorial director. Mike was a thoughtful and creative partner throughout the process—pushing for clarity, sharpening the narrative, and ensuring the ideas were both accessible and impactful.

I am deeply appreciative of the leaders across Omnicom Public Relations (OPR) who contributed their perspectives and experiences. Jim Margolis at GMMB, Terry Nelson at PLUS Communications, Simon Whitehead at Portland Public Affairs, and Robin Callif at OPR all provided invaluable input that helped ground this work in the realities of leadership, influence, and reputation in practice.

I also thank the client partners who generously shared their time and insights. Anton Vincent at Mars and Leslie McGibbon at British Telecom offered thoughtful reflections on leadership and reputation, drawing from their own experiences navigating complexity and change. Their contributions added important depth and perspective to this book.

Finally, and most important, I thank my family. Their support, patience, and encouragement through the inevitable ups and downs of this journey made this work possible. Without them, none of this would hold the same meaning.

This book reflects a collective effort, and I am grateful to all who contributed to its development.

INTRODUCTION

The Age of Exposure

We live in an age of exposure. Every decision is public, every action traceable, every inconsistency discoverable. Radical transparency is not coming; it is already here. Privacy, as we once knew it, is gone. But visibility is not the enemy of reputation. It is the proving ground.

In this environment, reputation becomes the most reliable form of truth. You cannot fake it for long. The market and the culture always find you out. And that is why reputation is not a defensive mechanism. It is a strategic engine of propulsion. It does more than protect. It accelerates. It builds resilience, opens doors, and creates momentum that money alone cannot buy.

Reputation as Propulsion

Over the years, I have seen what happens when organizations treat reputation as an afterthought, a "nice to have" delegated to the PR team. I have also seen what happens when leaders put it at the center of strategy. The difference is dramatic.

When reputation drives decision-making, people inside the

organization act differently. They think longer term. They collaborate better. They measure outcomes not only by profit and loss but by alignment and belief. Reputation becomes the operating system for growth, the guiding force that powers credibility, culture, and performance.

I often tell clients that if your marketing does not connect, your sales will not convert. And if your reputation is broken, both will suffer. Reputation is the quiet multiplier behind everything that works: your ability to attract talent, earn partnerships, secure investment, and win in a crowded marketplace.

And the data confirms it. In multiple industries from finance to technology, healthcare to hospitality, analysts estimate that reputation accounts for 30 to 50 percent of brand equity. In practical terms, that is billions in enterprise value, earned or lost.

From Intuition to Intelligence

Here is the good news: Reputation is not mysterious. We can measure it with precision. We can track sentiment in real time. We can see where perception is forming, which narratives are rising, and which signals carry emotional weight.

This is what I call reputation intelligence, the ability to convert cultural noise into strategic signals. It is not about surveillance. It is about awareness. It is the discipline of seeing yourself as the world sees you through the lens of data, behavior, and story.

Reputation has become the most important feedback loop in business. Every comment, click, review, and meme is a data point. Some signals are loud, like a viral post or a breaking headline.

Others are quiet, such as a shift in employee sentiment, a drop in customer patience, or a change in tone from partners or investors. Together they form a living map of perception.

When leaders study these signals carefully, they begin to understand reputation not as something to manage but as something to map, model, and act on.

Organizations that interpret these feedback loops early, and that can separate noise from narrative, are the ones that move fastest. They do not react to volatility. They harness it. They listen for what patterns predict, not just what they describe.

Reputation intelligence turns intuition into evidence. It separates organizations that react from those that anticipate.

The Human Core

Yet even with all the analytics, this is still a human story. Reputation lives in emotion, in belonging and shared meaning. When people feel connected to your purpose, they forgive mistakes. When they feel misled or excluded, they walk away.

The companies that thrive are the ones that treat reputation as a relationship, not a transaction. They listen, adapt, and act with courage. They build cultures that echo their promises from the boardroom to the front line. And they empower leaders at every level to model the values that define the brand.

Throughout my career, I have worked with CEOs and senior leaders who understand this intuitively. They know that every interaction, whether a speech, a post, or a partnership, adds to or subtracts from the reputation account. Over time, the balance compounds. And when crisis comes, that equity becomes a safety net.

A company with deep reputation equity can stumble and recover. A company without it can look strong on paper and still fail.

Why I Wrote This Book

I wrote *The Reputation Advantage* to help leaders rethink reputation as a strategic discipline rather than a communications task. It is a field manual for a new era of business, one where perception moves faster than production and every stakeholder has a microphone.

You will read about leaders who turned reputation into leverage and about those who lost everything because they missed early signals. You will see how micro-moments, fandoms, and digital culture shape modern credibility. And you will learn how to measure, build, and protect reputation capital—the stored value of consistent behavior, visible integrity, and earned belief.

The chapters that follow draw on decades of global experience, from crisis management to campaign strategy, from boardrooms to social platforms. You will find frameworks, data-driven insights, and examples of what works and what does not.

You will also meet communicators, innovators, and leaders whose stories show how reputation, used with intention, becomes a force multiplier for growth.

Looking Ahead

In a world where attention is scarce and authenticity is priceless, reputation is the bridge between what you promise and what people believe. It is the currency that endures when markets shift or algorithms change. It follows you into every negotiation, partnership, and conversation.

My goal is to give you the tools to strengthen that bridge, to make it strong enough to support your ambitions and flexible enough to adapt to change. Today, reputation is not a static quality. It is a performance. Every leader, every brand, every organization is on stage every day. You cannot script the plot, but you can define your character.

The next chapters explore how signals, micro-moments, and emotional resonance shape reputational gravity. We look at how data, design, and leadership combine to build credibility at the speed of culture, influencing everything from a company's permission to operate to its stock price and its right to lead.

Reputation once grew slowly over the years. Now it can rise or collapse overnight. Markets move at tweet speed. Algorithms amplify everything, from mistakes to memes, from flashes of glory to moments of despair. One moment you are a headline, the next a hashtag. The question is not whether your reputation will be tested but when, and whether you are ready to respond with clarity, courage, and coherence.

Part I

REPUTATION AS ENTERPRISE STRATEGY

Chapter 1

TRUST IS BROKEN; REPUTATION IS THE ANTIDOTE

In a global culture in which trust is missing or greatly diminished, reputation has emerged as a sort of "universal antidote" to overcoming skepticism and suspicion. Reputation is a catalyst for sales; it's a foundation for building strong business relationships and elevating lifetime customer value, a key measure of long-term profitability. In today's digital marketplaces, consumers frequently make purchasing decisions based on collective opinions rather than on their trust in a brand. A strong reputation can be a powerful driver of behavior. It helps attract investors, retain loyal customers, engage talented employees, and foster communities and thought leadership around a brand.

Our research shows that people often buy from brands with a good reputation, even if they don't fully trust them. In fact, nearly nine in ten consumers regularly consult online reviews before purchasing.[1]

Personal influence also plays a major role. Family, friends, brand ambassadors, and especially visible leaders like the CEO can shape consumer perceptions, positively or negatively. This influence applies to both quick, intuitive purchases and more deliberate decisions. In either case, people are more likely to choose brands that reflect their values and that they feel proud to associate with.

For example, the CEO's reputation at the back of the consumer's mind will act as a nudge whenever they interact with the brand. Consumers may naturally gravitate toward a product or company that is linked to a strong, recognizable leader. They trust the leader's vision, values, and decision-making, even without direct interaction with the brand. This phenomenon, known as the halo effect, occurs when a company and its CEO become closely intertwined, each reinforcing the other's reputation and brand identity. For example, Richard Branson is strongly associated with Virgin and its sense of adventure. Similarly, Bernard Arnault and the Arnault family are deeply entwined with LVMH and its "maisons," reinforcing strong associations with luxury.

Brands want to be "trusted," yet most aren't. Nevertheless, brands are still selling products and services, which tells me that for many companies, trust is not the ultimate driver of sales or brand equity. On the other hand, the evidence linking reputation and sales is strong.

Let's pause for a moment for a quick review of the basics:

- *Brand* is built based on the alignment of brand promise and your ability to deliver on that promise.

- *Reputation* is a collection of beliefs based on perceptions—your perceptions and the perceptions of others.
- *Trust* is the outcome of positive experiences over time.

So which is most important: brand, reputation, or trust? Which deserves your full focus and primary attention? All three are important! Brand, reputation, and trust are interrelated and codependent. And yes, there is a logical sequence: You start by delivering consistently on your brand promise, which builds your reputation, which, in turn, enhances your reputation and builds trust in your brand. Rinse and repeat, ad infinitum. We look at many examples of this process throughout the book.

In a low-trust environment, a strong positive reputation opens doors for trial and creates opportunities. Here's an example: Recently I wanted to buy a new portable speaker online. After searching for the "10 best portable speakers" and reading endless charts and reviews, I was directed to a brand I'd never heard of before, and I bought their speaker. Do I "trust" this brand? No, I don't. But I trust the 2,324 reviews that gave it five stars, even though I've never met any of the people who wrote them. (The speaker is terrific, by the way!)

Brand and trust matter, but reputation is often the fastest and most effective driver of business impact. A strong reputation doesn't just attract attention; it accelerates engagement, builds loyalty, sparks sales, and fuels growth. Companies should cultivate all three, but reputation is the lever that moves results most quickly.

Several years ago, I wrote *Reputation Strategy and Analytics in a Hyper-Connected World*, a book in which I examine and describe numerous changes that were forcing us to rethink our approach to building, maintaining, nurturing, and capitalizing on reputation as a business driver. I also made two predictions that have proven accurate:

1. *New reputation-based markets will transform business, commerce, and society.* When was the last time you bought something without checking reviews, online rankings, or word of mouth?
2. *Digital and analytic functions will no longer sit as stand-alone departments.* AI is being built into everything; it will tell us where our reputation is faltering and provide guidance for improving it.

In this new book, we explore why and how reputation drives business success. We examine strategies for leveraging reputation to grow revenue, expand into new markets, and strengthen stakeholder relationships. By treating reputation as a core business asset, companies can build resilience, secure competitive advantage, and position their brands for lasting impact. Smart leaders understand that reputation is not just protection. It is propulsion.

TAKEAWAYS

- *Measure* your reputation quarterly with hard data (reviews, sentiment, stakeholder surveys)—don't wait for annual reports.

- *Tie* executive incentives to reputation performance as tightly as to financial outcomes.
- *Invest* in reputation equity the way you invest in R&D—as capital that compounds.
- *Build* a "reputation reserve" of advocates, partners, and proof points to deploy in crisis.
- *Reward* leaders who grow reputation as visibly as those who grow revenue.

Chapter 2

REPUTATION CAPITAL, BRAND EQUITY, AND BRAND VALUE

Reputation capital, brand equity, and brand value describe different forces operating within the same system. Together, they shape how organizations are perceived and judged over time. Yet these terms are often used casually, especially in moments of pressure, as if they were interchangeable. They are related, but for reputation leaders, the distinctions matter. Each behaves differently, and each exerts influence in a distinct way. For clarity, here are brief descriptions of the three forces:

- *Reputation capital* reflects accumulated stakeholder opinion shaped by what people observe about leadership decisions, behavior, and consistency.
- *Brand equity* reflects experience: promise made, promise kept across products, services, and touchpoints.

- *Brand value* reflects how financial markets quantify those signals, including preference, pricing power, and perceived future potential.

Reputation capital sustains belief, particularly when expectations are tested. Brand equity creates familiarity, preference, and recognition. When the two reinforce one another, brand value is strengthened. When they drift out of alignment, brand value becomes more fragile.

Brand experience matters deeply, but reputation capital influences how that experience is interpreted when conditions change. It affects whether stakeholders maintain their expectations or begin to reassess what they believe about the brand.

The Reputation Economy in Practice

The idea of a reputation economy emerged because traditional brand models could not fully explain how decisions were actually being made. Entire industries have formed around reputation as a primary decision mechanism rather than as a by-product of experience. Platforms like eBay and Uber did not succeed simply because of technology or convenience. They worked because reputation systems created accountability and confidence between people who had no prior relationship. Rating mechanisms were not add-ons or marketing features. They were foundational infrastructure that made confidence scalable.

What emerged was not just a new way of making decisions, but a new way of assigning value based on confidence rather than proximity or experience alone. That same logic now operates far beyond digital platforms. Investors evaluate leadership credibility as much as strategy. Employees choose employers based on perceived alignment and behavior. Regulators assess intent as well as compliance. Customers decide whether to forgive mistakes based on what they believe an organization stands for and how it has behaved in the past. Reputation has become a connective force that shapes decisions before experience occurs and continues to influence judgment long after.

There is no equivalent "brand economy" in quite the same way. Brand experience is deeply personal and contextual. It is shaped through direct interaction, memory, and emotion. Reputation, by contrast, is collective and portable. It travels ahead of experience and frames how experience is interpreted once it happens. That difference explains why reputation can move faster than brand experience, and why it often becomes decisive when time horizons compress.

Related, but Not Interchangeable

We often say that brands have reputations, which is true. We do not say that reputations have brands. That asymmetry is revealing. Brand lives inside the organization's promise architecture. It is designed, articulated, and delivered through products and experiences. Reputation lives outside the organization. It is formed through observation, interpretation, and shared judgment. Brand is something an organization builds and delivers. Reputation is something it earns and sustains.

Confusion tends to arise when marketing and public relations are treated as interchangeable disciplines. They are not. They operate on different timelines, with different tools and different constraints. Marketing is exceptional at building brand experiences that scale. It orchestrates product, pricing, distribution, storytelling, and design across the enterprise. Its work is cumulative, operational, and deeply integrated into how the organization functions.

Public relations (PR) operates in a different environment. It works in real time, under scrutiny, often with incomplete information and little margin for error. PR earns attention rather than buying it, and it does so in public view, frequently when stakes are highest and expectations are least forgiving. Both disciplines matter. Both contribute to value. But collapsing them into a single, vague idea of "brand reputation" obscures their distinct roles and weakens their effectiveness.

A strong brand reputation generates preference and resilience; it gives organizations elbow room to operate in crowded and competitive markets. When marketers talk about "brand equity," brand reputation is often what they mean. But in capital markets, the word *equity* implies ownership, valuation, and quantification. Both meanings are useful, as long as we are clear about context.

When marketers talk about brand equity, what we usually mean is the advantage created by familiarity, consistency, and experience. Strong brand equity shows up in preference, loyalty, pricing power, and a degree of resilience that comes only from repeated delivery over time. It is slow to build because it depends on experience. Once established, it is also relatively forgiving. A brand that has delivered reliably for years can disappoint occasionally without losing its place in the customer's mind.

Reputation capital is built differently, and it plays a different role. It reflects accumulated stakeholder opinion shaped by observable leadership behavior rather than experience alone. Reputation capital accumulates through alignment between what leaders say and what organizations do, especially when conditions are uncertain and scrutiny is unavoidable. It reflects how an organization behaves under pressure, how consistently it applies its values, and whether its actions reinforce or undermine its stated direction. Over time, it becomes a reserve of credibility that organizations draw on when expectations are tested.

I am cautious about treating these forces as neat line items on a balance sheet, even though markets and financial reporting often attempt to quantify parts of them. But markets behave as if they are real, and stakeholders respond to them as tangible forces. Investors, employees, regulators, and customers make decisions based on confidence, and confidence is shaped by behavior. In that sense, reputation capital and brand equity may not show up on formal balance sheets, but they are continuously priced in. Brand value is the expression of that pricing.

Not a Sequence but a Situation

Executives sometimes ask me to help them prioritize reputation capital, brand equity, and brand value. The instinct behind their questions is understandable, but it assumes a sequence that rarely exists. It would be a mistake to impose hierarchy or sequence on these forces; they operate simultaneously, with different effects depending on timing, pressure, and visibility.

Before deciding where to invest effort, leaders need to understand what is actually under stress. A decline in sales, a loss of relevance, competitive pressure, leadership credibility, and market confidence are different problems, even when they are discussed using the same language. Until that distinction is clear, choosing between brand and reputation is largely theoretical, and leaders risk misallocating effort at the moment when value is most exposed.

If the goal is to build long-term preference, enter new markets, or redefine a category, brand experience is foundational. That work takes time. It requires coordination across functions and consistent delivery over years, not quarters. It is, by nature, a long-term commitment.

If the organization is on the clock, facing scrutiny, managing uncertainty, or responding to pressure, reputation capital moves faster. It is more dynamic, more sensitive to leadership behavior, and more immediately consequential. Brand experience changes slowly because it is built across products, systems, and people. Reputation moves more quickly because it is shaped by visible decisions and public behavior. When time horizons shrink, reputation often becomes the more responsive instrument.

Put simply, it is faster and often easier to influence reputation than it is to reshape brand experience. Reputation work registers immediately. Brand work compounds over time. That difference explains why reputation capital so often becomes the decisive factor when organizations are under pressure.

This is why reputation capital frequently converts under pressure. When conditions are calm, brand equity does much of the work. When conditions tighten, history matters more than promise, and behavior carries more weight than messaging.

How Value Is Sustained

Value holds up under pressure when brand equity and reputation capital reinforce one another, maintaining market confidence even as conditions become more demanding. Brand equity contributes visibility, familiarity, and preference. Reputation capital contributes credibility, confidence, and resilience. Together, they shape how stakeholders assess future potential.

Market signals often tell us less about current performance than about belief. Stock price, in particular, functions as a confidence indicator. It reflects how credible a strategy appears, whether leadership is believed capable of execution, and whether stakeholders expect the organization to deliver what it has said it will deliver. Reputation capital plays an outsize role in shaping that belief, especially when results are uneven or the path forward is still being tested.

When brand equity outpaces reputation capital, visibility can become vulnerability. When reputation capital reinforces brand equity, value holds steady, even when performance fluctuates. The alignment between what an organization promises and how it behaves determines whether value compounds or weakens.

For leaders, the implication is practical rather than theoretical. Brand equity cannot be rushed. Reputation capital cannot be deferred. Both require deliberate management, with a clear understanding of when each one matters most.

In the end, this is less about adopting a framework than about exercising judgment, recognizing which force is exerting the greatest influence in the moment, and responding accordingly.

In an environment defined by transparency, speed, and constant judgment, reputation capital has become a strategic asset. It does not replace brand experience. It determines whether brand experience is believed and supported when expectations are tested. That is the relationship leaders need to understand, not as a set of rules to memorize, but as guidance for decisions made when confidence is at stake.

TAKEAWAYS

- *Understand the three forces at work.* Distinguish clearly among reputation capital, brand equity, and brand value, and recognize how each one contributes differently to enterprise value.
- *Diagnose before you act.* Identify whether you are addressing a long-term brand equity issue or a short-term reputation capital challenge; then apply the appropriate lever.
- *Build brand equity patiently.* Invest in consistent experiences across products, services, and touchpoints, recognizing that brand equity compounds over time rather than delivering immediate results.
- *Deploy reputation capital deliberately.* In moments of scrutiny or uncertainty, focus leadership attention on visible decisions and behaviors that reinforce stated priorities and direction.
- *Treat reputation as a leadership asset.* Reputational evaluation metrics should be factored into decision-making.

- *Test alignment regularly*. Compare what the organization promises publicly with how it behaves operationally, especially during moments that attract attention or external evaluation.

Chapter 3

REPUTATION: THE CAPITAL YOU CAN'T IGNORE

Reputation has always mattered in business, but in today's markets, it's something companies can bank, invest, and deploy strategically. Reputation is a form of capital that lowers barriers to entry. When a brand has strong reputation equity, customers extend it the benefit of the doubt, regulators trust its motives, and employees align with its mission. In practical terms, that means a company with a strong reputation can move faster into new markets, launch riskier innovations, and withstand occasional missteps without suffering catastrophic damage.

Reputation equity reframes reputation from a vague, feel-good concept into a measurable and tradable resource. Just as financial equity provides the foundation for growth, reputation equity is the capital a company accumulates over time. It's built through consistent delivery of quality and visible alignment between what a brand says and what it does.

Think of it as capital that can be traded on. Brands that have invested in their reputation can draw from that reserve to introduce new products, ask customers for patience when something goes wrong, or gain market entry ahead of less-known rivals. Apple is a familiar example. The delight of opening its packaging, the seamless reliability of its devices, and bold decisions such as Tim Cook's refusal to compromise customer privacy all reinforce a reservoir of reputation equity. That reservoir cushions the brand in tough moments and accelerates its ability to expand.

Apple is just one instance of this phenomenon. Brands across multiple industries have taken advantage of their reputation equity to help them build back from weak positions or seize new opportunities. For example:

- *Toyota's reputation for reliability* gave the company room to rebound after a series of safety recalls. Because customers trusted the brand's long-term commitment to quality, they viewed the crisis as a temporary setback rather than a permanent failure.

- *Patagonia's consistent focus on sustainability* has been reinforced through decades of aligned products, policies, and activism. That steady approach has built reputation equity strong enough to win loyalty at premium prices and differentiate the brand in a crowded outdoor market.

- *Warby Parker* built reputation equity around transparency and social impact from the start. That foundation allowed the company to scale while keeping customer goodwill firmly intact.

- *Microsoft, under Satya Nadella,* rebuilt its reputation by embracing openness, collaboration, and a growth mindset. That turnaround restored trust with developers, regulators, and enterprise customers, giving the company the equity to expand aggressively into cloud and AI markets.

These examples show how reputation equity works as universal capital for growth and resilience. But reputation equity can also erode if it's not maintained. Unlike financial capital, it can't be stored in a vault and left alone. Reputation equity demands ongoing deposits—daily acts of consistency, responsiveness, and innovation. Fail to maintain it, and the "interest rate" turns negative: Consumers grow skeptical, employees disengage, and expansion slows.

The fragility of reputation isn't just visible in corporate case studies. It has become a recurring theme in popular culture. Stories and cautionary tales remind us how quickly reputations can be made, manipulated, or destroyed.

Reputation scores don't just track popularity; they determine whose voices carry weight. That echoes how today's celebrities and influencers dominate attention. A single endorsement, review, or cancellation from someone influential can significantly affect markets and consumer behavior, converting symbolic approval directly into tangible business value.

We've also internalized surveillance, curating our conduct under the constant fear of judgment. Goodhart's Law reminds us that when a measure becomes a target—whether reputation scores, follower counts, or stock valuations—it loses meaning and begins to distort behavior. Together, these examples show why reputation, once a by-product of value creation, has become a currency in its own right: tradable, leveraged, and, at times, weaponized.

TAKEAWAYS

- *Audit* your reputation equity regularly; identify reserves of goodwill and areas of vulnerability.
- *Invest* in consistent delivery, transparency, and alignment; these are the deposits that grow equity.
- *Leverage* strong equity to accelerate launches, enter new markets, or recover from missteps.
- *Monitor* for erosion; treat lapses in consistency as withdrawals that weaken your balance sheet.
- *Build* equity daily through small, credible actions, not just headline campaigns.

Chapter 4

PERMISSION TO MARKET IS EARNED, NOT BOUGHT

One of the most underappreciated truths in our industry is that reputation is permission to market. A brand can have the most inventive ad campaign in the world, but if the public questions its credibility or rejects the very premise of the product, the campaign will fail before it starts.

Marketing focuses on brand preference, explaining why someone should choose your product over another. PR focuses on brand permission, explaining why you have the right to be in the conversation at all. You can't have one without the other. Before people can decide to prefer you, they must first decide to accept you. That acceptance is earned over time through actions, consistency, and alignment between what you say and what you do.

This is why PR is not a luxury. So don't put it in the "nice to have" box to be opened only when the budget allows; use its power as the foundation that makes marketing possible. Without the credibility that effective PR builds, marketing has no traction. PR shapes the environment so marketing can succeed.

Actions That Speak

Some of the most effective reputation strategies in recent years have come from brands making bold, creative choices aligned with their values:

- *Patagonia's* decision to redirect Black Friday profits to grassroots environmental groups
- *Airbnb's* program offering free housing to displaced refugees
- *Ben & Jerry's* producing shareable, visually bold explainers on social justice issues
- *IKEA's "ThisAbles"* 3D-printable accessibility add-ons
- *Heineken's "Worlds Apart"* social experiment pairing strangers with opposing views
- *LEGO's "Replay"* program repurposing used bricks for underserved children
- *Cleveland Clinic's "Empathy"* video series, centered on patient and staff humanity
- *NVIDIA's AI Art Gallery*, showcasing art created with its AI tools

These weren't just campaigns; they were creative acts of alignment. Each reinforced the brand's core identity while inviting audiences to engage with meaning rather than just messaging.

Even smaller gestures, like turning a product recall into a moment of transparency or engaging real employees instead of actors in employer branding, can creatively reshape public perception. These decisions require courage and cultural awareness. And they work because they don't just protect reputation; they *amplify it* through creative action.

Product launches can also be reputational turning points. In 1984, Nike was struggling to find its footing in basketball. Adidas and Converse dominated the court, and Nike's market share was slipping. Instead of playing it safe, Nike made a creative leap: betting on an unproven rookie named Michael Jordan. What made the deal radical wasn't just the endorsement; it was the contract itself. Negotiated by Jordan's mother, Deloris, it gave him a percentage of every Air Jordan sold, flipping the traditional athlete–brand relationship on its head.[1]

The gamble paid off. Nike had hoped to sell $3 million worth of shoes over the first couple of years. Instead, the Air Jordan line pulled in $126 million in the first year alone.[2] That bold move didn't just save Nike's basketball business; it redefined sports marketing and set the template for athlete–brand partnerships that followed. A reputational bet became a cultural shift and a reminder that sometimes creativity means being willing to break the old rules of the game.[3]

When Creativity Ripples Across Cultures

Ultimately, reputation is a story shaped by actions—and creativity is the force that imbues those actions with meaning. But creativity can stretch way beyond direct, planned impact and generate cultural ripples long after the original touchpoints. A compelling song from a video game or movie might spark an emotional attachment, turning a player or cinephile into a devoted fan of the band or composer. In 2025, *KPop Demon Hunters* exemplified this phenomenon: An animated movie featuring a fictional K-pop girl group, HUNTR/X, not only became Netflix's most-watched film ever but also saw its soundtrack explode globally, while winning Oscars for best animated feature and best original song for "Golden." The track "Golden" topped the Billboard Global 200, and multiple songs from the soundtrack charted simultaneously—outcomes certainly not part of the original marketing brief. This illustrates how creative brand experiences can spark real-world fandom and cultural momentum long after they launch.[4]

Consider *Kingdom Come: Deliverance*, a video game set in medieval Bohemia. Its rich historical details and immersive storytelling didn't just entertain; they sparked renewed tourism interest in the region. Today, destinations across modern Bohemia are seeing an influx of visitors inspired not by traditional travel campaigns but by the worlds they explored inside the game.[5] Regional tourism boards have since embraced this momentum, launching portals and cultural trails that link back to the game's narrative. Similar effects were seen with *Game of Thrones* in Northern Ireland and Croatia, *The Lord of the Rings* in New Zealand, and *Dracula* and *Wednesday* in Romania. In each case, what began as entertainment evolved into a catalyst for regional economic growth.

This is the long tail of creative reputation work. Beyond the memoir or documentary genre, a game designer's, book author's, or film director's decision to include a historical real-life location in the story becomes a reason for someone to book a holiday. A band's song, featured incidentally, becomes a gateway to a lifelong fan or the music choice for weddings. These are much more than momentary brand impressions; they're elements that form bigger, transformative life experiences. And while they may not start as PR or marketing, they're proof that when creativity resonates, it travels far beyond the campaign window.

Picking up the popular story and attracting a major film or game production is increasingly seen as potential for an economic development strategy. Behind the curtains of long-term success are often the efforts of national investment agencies that court production studios, offer tax incentives, and provide location support and logistical coordination, working hand in hand with other organizations and stakeholders on a global stage.

True brand reputation isn't just built—it can be an extended experience that is revisited and sometimes rediscovered in entirely new contexts.

TAKEAWAYS

- *Recognize* reputation as your license to operate and your permission to market; without credibility, even the most inventive campaigns fail.
- *Use* PR to establish permission before deploying marketing; preference only matters once acceptance is secured.

- *Invest* in creative acts of alignment—bold choices that reinforce values and invite engagement.
- *Seize* product launches and cultural moments as reputational turning points; bold bets create lasting permission.
- *Anticipate* ripple effects—when creativity resonates, it can generate cultural and even economic momentum far beyond the campaign window.

Chapter 5

REPUTATION OPENS THE DOOR; TRUST KEEPS YOU IN THE ROOM

Trust and reputation influence how organizations are perceived, but the pace and pattern of how perception develops have changed. The environment is more transparent, more participatory, and more volatile than ever before. A single signal, whether accurate or distorted, can travel across platforms before an organization has a chance to respond. Stakeholders do not wait for the official version of a story. They form judgments quickly, based on whatever signals are most visible.

This shift creates a new hierarchy of perception. Reputation emerges first because it is shaped by collective signals that appear ahead of any direct experience. Someone learns about a company through a comment thread, a review, a headline, or a conversation with a friend before they interact with the brand itself. These signals create the frame through which trust may eventually develop, but trust cannot form until a relationship begins. Reputation must therefore carry the initial burden of credibility.

Leaders sometimes underestimate how quickly reputation forms. They focus on internal strengths, brand narratives, and experience design without recognizing that most stakeholders encounter the company indirectly. A potential customer may see a review before reading a marketing message. A regulator may remember a past incident before assessing a new filing. An investor may watch leadership behavior before reviewing quarterly performance. These interactions shape reputation long before trust has a chance to emerge.

This is why reputation deserves dedicated attention. It determines who is willing to enter the conversation. Trust determines who will stay in the conversation once it begins. Organizations that rely on trust alone assume that every stakeholder has already given them a chance to prove themselves. That assumption no longer holds. Reputation is now the gateway to engagement.

For companies that operate in regulated environments, competitive markets, or high-visibility sectors, this shift is especially significant. Reputation influences how regulators interpret compliance, how communities respond to development, how investors weigh risk, and how talent evaluates opportunity. Trust cannot perform these functions at scale because trust is built one relationship at a time. Reputation scales because it is shaped through signals that reach many stakeholders simultaneously.

This reality forces leaders to adopt a new mindset. Reputation is not a passive outcome. It is a managed system. It must be shaped intentionally, strengthened consistently, and protected proactively. Trust is equally important, but it cannot be manufactured or accelerated. It must be earned through experiences that reinforce the promises the reputation system has already set in motion.

The distinction matters now because the environment demands precision. When leaders confuse trust with reputation, they design strategies that are too slow to respond to modern expectations. They invest in trust programs that never gain traction because stakeholders have not yet experienced the organization directly. They rely on messaging instead of alignment. They react to scrutiny instead of preparing for it. They look for loyalty before establishing credibility.

The companies that thrive in this environment understand that trust and reputation work together, but they do not work the same way. Each serves a distinct purpose. Each requires distinct investments. Each responds to different types of signals. Understanding this distinction is no longer optional. It is fundamental to modern leadership.

This is why it is essential to understand clearly the distinction between trust and reputation, because each requires different management and different types of evidence to be effective.

Defining the Terms

Trust and reputation are related but fundamentally different concepts. They intersect, influence each other, and share certain qualities, yet they serve different functions in the architecture of stakeholder perception.

Trust is personal. It is built slowly through repeated interactions and consistent delivery. It depends on individual experiences.

An employee trusts leadership because leaders make fair decisions and communicate openly. A customer trusts a product because it performs reliably. A regulator trusts a company because it demonstrates compliance over time. These judgments vary across stakeholder groups because each group interacts with the company differently.

Trust also carries emotional weight. It reflects how stakeholders feel about the relationship. When trust is strong, people are willing to give the organization the benefit of the doubt. They accept occasional imperfections because the broader pattern supports confidence. When trust is shaken, people withdraw quickly because the emotional foundation has shifted. Trust grows carefully, yet it breaks abruptly.

Reputation functions differently. It is collective rather than personal. It reflects the combined effect of the signals that stakeholders observe, whether or not they have experienced the brand personally. These signals include performance, leadership behavior, media coverage, public commentary, product reliability, workplace culture, and third-party assessments. Reputation synthesizes these signals into a broad judgment about credibility.

Reputation is inferred, not experienced. People form reputational judgments before they interact with the company directly. They look at reviews, headlines, or peer experiences to decide whether an organization is worth their time. Reputation is also transferable. A leader with a strong reputation can influence perception at a new company. A brand with a strong reputation can enter a new market more quickly than a brand without one. Trust does not travel in this way because trust must be earned through direct experience.

Despite their differences, trust and reputation share important qualities. Neither is owned by the company. Both exist in the minds of stakeholders. Both can act as shock absorbers in crisis. Both require consistent behavior to maintain. Yet these shared qualities should not obscure the distinctions that drive strategy. Reputation forms first. Trust forms later. Reputation operates at scale. Trust operates through relationships. Reputation drives initial action. Trust drives long-term resilience.

Leaders who understand these differences can design systems that build each force on its own terms. They invest in the signals that shape reputation. They support the behaviors that earn trust. They measure each separately. They treat each as a tool with distinct value. The result is a more complete, more effective approach to perception management.

The Sequence That Governs Behavior

Trust does not precede reputation. Reputation precedes trust. This sequence is not philosophical. It is observable in every stakeholder journey.

A customer does not trust a product before forming a reputational judgment about it. They read reviews, check ratings, and consider the credibility of the company. These signals shape the decision to try the product in the first place. Only after using it repeatedly does the customer begin to form trust.

An employee does not trust leadership before developing a reputational sense of how the organization treats its people. They look at workplace culture, turnover patterns, public commentary, and the behavior of leaders under pressure. Reputation shapes whether they join. Experience shapes whether they stay.

A regulator does not trust a company before assessing its reputational record in compliance, governance, or community impact. Reputation shapes the lens through which new requests are evaluated. Trust grows only after repeated alignment between expectation and behavior.

This sequence matters because it guides investment. Leaders sometimes attempt to build trust through campaigns, narratives, or targeted programs before establishing a strong reputation foundation. These initiatives struggle because trust cannot be accelerated through messaging. Stakeholders need evidence, not claims. They need experience, not aspiration. Without that foundation, trust-building becomes a slow and expensive effort.

When organizations focus first on reputation, they create the conditions in which trust can form more easily. Stakeholders enter the relationship expecting reliability. They give the organization more space to prove itself. They interpret early experiences more positively. Reputation smooths the path to trust.

When organizations focus first on trust, they often find themselves pushing against an unreceptive environment. Stakeholders are not ready to grant the benefit of the doubt. They question messages rather than accepting them. They need reputational proof before they are willing to engage emotionally.

The sequence is therefore simple: Define the promise, build reputation by demonstrating credibility, and earn trust through consistency. This approach respects how stakeholders actually behave. It aligns strategy with reality. It ensures that both reputation and trust grow from the right foundations.

The Measurement Gap

Measurement is often where the confusion between trust and reputation becomes clear. Trust is usually measured through surveys that ask stakeholders how much confidence they have in the organization. These surveys capture sentiment, which is important for understanding the emotional dimension of relationships. However, trust surveys are useful for measuring attitudes and stated intentions, but by themselves, they typically do not show how an organization's standing actually changes real-world behavior.

Reputation can be measured more directly through behavioral and financial indicators that reveal how stakeholders actually respond. Stakeholders who view a company as reputable tend to act differently. They buy more readily. They stay longer. They recover faster from moments of disappointment. Markets respond differently to companies with strong reputations. Investors require lower risk premiums. Regulators grant more flexibility. Customers are less sensitive to price. These outcomes can be quantified.

Reputation equity describes the value created by this pattern. When reputation is strong, the organization gains economic advantages. When reputation declines, the organization faces new costs and constraints. These effects appear consistently across industries. Reputation influences the speed and scale of opportunity. Trust influences the depth and durability of relationships.

Leaders need both types of measurements, but they must interpret each correctly. Trust scores explain part of the picture. Reputation data explains another part. Neither tells the whole story alone. Together, they give leaders a more complete understanding of how stakeholders make decisions and how those decisions affect the company.

To manage reputation effectively, leaders must treat it like capital rather than sentiment. They must evaluate the signals that influence stakeholders, the systems that produce those signals, and the outcomes those signals generate. They must integrate measurement across brand, policy, purpose, product, and performance. They must recognize that reputation is dynamic, not static. It changes with new information, new experiences, and new expectations.

Trust must be measured differently. It requires monitoring the stability of relationships, the consistency of delivery, and the reliability of commitments. Trust measurement is slower, but it reveals important patterns about loyalty, engagement, and risk.

When leaders separate these measurements, they can shape strategy with greater precision. They can strengthen the signals that influence reputation. They can support the behaviors that build trust. They can build a more resilient organization that performs well in both stable and turbulent conditions.

Reputation Acts as a Stabilizer

Crises reveal the difference between trust and reputation more clearly than any other moment. When something goes wrong, trust often evaporates first. Stakeholders respond emotionally. They feel disappointed or misled. Their confidence in the relationship weakens. Trust that took years to build can break in hours.

Reputation, however, often holds even when trust falters. Because reputation is built from a broad range of signals, it tends to withstand individual failures. A company with a strong reputation can endure a crisis with less damage than a company with a weak reputation. Stakeholders who respect the company's overall performance are more likely to grant it space to explain. Regulators are more likely to interpret the incident as an exception rather than a pattern. Investors are more likely to focus on long-term value rather than immediate disruption.

Reputation acts as a stabilizer. It gives leaders time to respond. It keeps stakeholders engaged. It reduces the likelihood of rapid escalation. It protects the organization from the full consequences of a single failure.

Trust returns only after leaders demonstrate consistent improvement over time. Reputation returns more quickly because it depends on signals that steady once the crisis ends. Leaders who understand this dynamic invest heavily in reputation long before any crisis occurs. They build credibility in advance so they have a buffer when they need it most.

The organizations that recover fastest from crises are those that understand the difference between trust and reputation. They communicate clearly, act decisively, and reinforce alignment across signals. They rebuild trust by demonstrating reliability. They rebuild reputation by restoring confidence in their overall direction. They treat crisis as both a test and an opportunity to demonstrate leadership.

Trust as Human Capital; Reputation as Strategic Capital

Trust and reputation each create value, but they create value in different ways. Trust functions as human capital. It strengthens relationships, improves retention, stabilizes culture, and deepens customer loyalty. Trust makes stakeholders willing to engage, forgive, and advocate. It enhances the quality of relationships. It supports long-term resilience.

Reputation functions as strategic capital. It drives market behavior, influences external decisions, and shapes enterprise value. Reputation affects how quickly opportunities appear, how readily partners commit, and how confidently investors act. It influences pricing, acquisition costs, regulatory posture, and the company's ability to navigate uncertainty. Reputation accelerates progress. Trust amplifies it.

Organizations need both. Reputation gives companies access. Trust gives them continuity. Reputation determines the speed at which the company can move. Trust determines the strength with which it can endure. Reputation is the catalyst. Trust is the anchor.

Leaders who treat reputation as strategic capital invest in systems that create alignment across the enterprise. They focus on coherence between message and behavior. They integrate brand, policy, purpose, product, and performance into a unified perception. They measure reputation continually and adjust strategy based on how signals are changing.

Leaders who treat trust as human capital focus on consistent delivery. They support managers, improve culture, and reinforce commitments. They engage stakeholders directly. They ensure actions reflect values. They understand that trust takes time and cannot be rushed.

The two forms of capital are connected, but they are not identical. Organizations that conflate them miss opportunities to strengthen each one. Organizations that manage them separately build competitive advantage.

AI Rebalances the Equation

Artificial intelligence (AI) accelerates perception. It amplifies signals, identifies inconsistencies, and highlights gaps between expectation and performance. In an AI-driven environment, reputation becomes even more significant. AI does not wait for context. It does not wait for explanation. It surfaces patterns instantly. Leaders cannot rely on manual reputation management. They need systems that ensure coherence across every part of the organization.

AI makes it harder to sustain reputational illusions. Messaging that once softened the impact of misalignment now collapses quickly under algorithmic scrutiny. Stakeholders have access to more information, more quickly and from more sources. They compare signals across channels. They expect consistency. They reward alignment and punish divergence.

Trust also becomes more complex in an AI-driven world. Stakeholders question the authenticity of messages. They question the integrity of processes. They question the reliability of information. This puts greater pressure on organizations to demonstrate reliability through action, not communication.

AI therefore intensifies the importance of treating reputation as a system and trust as an experience. Leadership must ensure that behavior matches message. They must ensure that the organization presents a coherent identity across all channels. AI will expose misalignment. Only alignment will protect the organization.

The companies that succeed in this environment are those that anticipate scrutiny. They build infrastructures that support coherence. They treat reputation as the connective tissue across the enterprise. They reinforce trust through repeated delivery. They use AI to monitor alignment, not manipulate perception.

They understand that authenticity and consistency are the only sustainable paths forward.

Building the New Playbook

Leaders who want to succeed in a world defined by transparency and acceleration must build an enterprise playbook that strengthens both reputation and trust. This requires clear priorities and disciplined execution.

Reputation must come first. Leaders must identify the signals that shape perception. These signals include product reliability, leadership behavior, workplace culture, public communication, and external visibility. Leaders must align these signals so they reinforce the same message. This requires cross-functional coordination. Reputation cannot be managed by one team alone. It requires alignment across every part of the organization.

Once reputation is established, leaders must invest in the behaviors that build trust. These behaviors are often more personal and experiential. They require consistency, transparency, and accountability. They require leaders to demonstrate reliability in moments of uncertainty. They require teams to deliver on the promises the organization has made.

The enterprise playbook must also include mechanisms for measurement. Leaders must track reputational signals in real time. They must evaluate trust through patterns of behavior, not just sentiment surveys. They must connect both forms of perceptions to economic outcomes so they can demonstrate value to boards and investors.

Finally, the enterprise playbook must include plans for crisis management. Leaders must understand how reputation and trust influence recovery. They must respond quickly to protect reputation and then rebuild trust through action. They must communicate clearly, act decisively, and maintain alignment across every signal. They must use crises as opportunities to demonstrate commitment to values and stakeholders.

Organizations that build this playbook gain a significant advantage. They move faster than competitors. They recover more effectively. They build stronger relationships. They create more durable value. They understand that trust and reputation are not interchangeable; they are interconnected forces that must be managed intentionally.

• • •

Trust and reputation are distinct forces that shape perception, behavior, and value. Reputation forms quickly through collective signals. Trust forms slowly through personal experience. Reputation opens opportunities. Trust sustains them. Reputation drives immediate action. Trust drives long-term loyalty. Leaders who treat them as interchangeable weaken their strategies. Leaders who treat them as separate but connected create clarity, resilience, and advantage.

The sequence is simple. Build reputation first by aligning signals across the enterprise. Then earn trust through reliable performance. Strengthen both over time through consistency and coherence. In an environment shaped by scrutiny and acceleration, this approach is not optional. It is essential for modern leadership.

Reputation is the catalyst and trust is the anchor. Leaders who manage both with intention are better prepared for a world defined by transparency and acceleration.

TAKEAWAYS

- *Strengthen reputation signals before investing in trust programs.* Build a foundation of credibility so stakeholders arrive open to forming trust.
- *Integrate brand, policy, purpose, product, and performance into one coherent system.* Align signals so reputation reflects real behavior rather than aspiration.
- *Use real-time measurement to track reputation and behavioral indicators to assess trust.* Evaluate each force through the metrics that best represent its value.
- *Prepare for crisis by building strong reputation equity early.* Create resilience that protects the enterprise when trust falters.
- *Build trust through consistent delivery and transparent communication.* Reinforce reliability through actions that match expectations.
- *Use AI as a tool for detecting alignment, not shaping illusion.* Ensure the story the organization tells is the story it lives.

Chapter 6

BUILT FOR THE STORM: LEADING WITH REPUTATION IN A CRISIS-DEFINED WORLD

Across industries, a familiar pattern shows up. Leaders emphasize growth and innovation but forget to prepare for disruption. And in today's transparent world, disruption is not unusual. It is expected. Crises rarely arrive slowly or through predictable channels. They come through social platforms, internal networks, sudden operational issues, misinformation loops, and cultural flashpoints. They influence decisions and alter perceptions long before official responses take shape.

This is why crisis management can no longer be treated as an emergency tool. It must be understood as a central part of reputation strategy. When a crisis hits, the public evaluates not only what happened but also who you are. They assess your values, your consistency, your presence, and your ability to communicate with calm and conviction. A crisis becomes a test of identity, and your response becomes the clearest expression of what you stand for.

Reputation is not something you protect only after the fact. It is something you build long before a crisis appears. It influences how much benefit of the doubt you receive, how quickly stakeholders support your decisions, and how effectively you can recover. In crisis moments, organizations draw on the trust they have earned over time.

This chapter explores how crisis management has evolved, why traditional approaches often fall short, and what it means to lead through a crisis with reputation at the center. Crisis work today is not only about limiting damage. It is about demonstrating identity, reinforcing values, and creating stability in moments of uncertainty.

From Crisis Response to Crisis Readiness

For years, crisis communications operated under the assumption that crises were rare. Leaders prepared binders, drafted scenarios, and conducted occasional drills. That world is gone. Crises now emerge from anywhere: a product concern, a political shift, a customer interaction that goes viral without context, an employee complaint, or an unexpected failure in a system that usually works.

The new environment demands readiness rather than reaction. Readiness is not just a plan. It is a posture. It is a way of operating that keeps the organization aware, connected, and responsive.

A readiness posture includes the following:

- Clear leadership roles

- Defined escalation pathways
- Rapid decision-making
- Open communication across teams
- Stakeholder mapping
- Real-time monitoring
- Messaging rooted in values

When leaders operate with readiness in mind, they build the muscle memory required to respond with confidence rather than fear. They reduce confusion and shorten the path to clarity.

Reputation as the Foundation of Crisis Strategy

Reputation is often treated as a measure of public sentiment. But in a crisis, reputation becomes structural. It shapes how people interpret your actions and how long they are willing to extend grace or patience.

When a crisis hits, the public instinctively asks:

- Is this consistent with who they say they are?
- Are they being honest?
- Are they acting responsibly?

- Do they understand the moment?
- Can they fix the problem?

This is why reputation pillars must guide crisis decisions. They determine tone, message, action, and outreach. For example, if transparency is a pillar, you cannot rely on vague language. If community is a pillar, you must engage key groups early. If innovation is a pillar, you must demonstrate forward movement. If accountability is a pillar, leadership must be visible and involved.

When your crisis response reflects your identity, people stay with you. When it contradicts your identity, people drift away.

Crisis Resistance: Strengthening the Organization Before Anything Happens

Crisis resistance begins with acknowledgment. You will face crises. The goal is not to avoid them entirely because that is impossible. The goal is to reduce their severity and shorten their duration.

Organizations must identify vulnerabilities across three dimensions: (1) operational vulnerabilities, (2) reputational vulnerabilities, and (3) cultural vulnerabilities. I encourage leaders to map these vulnerabilities through open and honest discussion. Ask your team these questions:

- What could go wrong?
- How likely is it?

- How visible would it be?
- How would stakeholders interpret it?
- What reputation themes would it activate?

Once identified, categorize risks by impact and likelihood. Some crises are high impact but unlikely. Others are highly likely but manageable. Some unfold slowly. Others appear all at once.

Building resistance also requires:

- A clear crisis structure
- Direct communication channels
- Defined leadership roles
- A culture that surfaces issues early
- Early warning systems built around listening rather than guessing

Leaders who build resistance create stability. They keep small issues from becoming large ones and prevent unforced errors from becoming defining events.

Crisis Responsiveness: What Happens When the Spotlight Arrives

When a crisis appears, speed becomes a proxy for competence. People want acknowledgment quickly. They do not expect full answers immediately, but they want assurance that leadership is aware, engaged, and taking action.

Every effective crisis response includes six components, which are outlined as follows: a defined crisis team, an immediate placeholder message, message architecture based on the five C's, stakeholder sequencing, real-time intelligence monitoring, and message discipline across channels.

A DEFINED CRISIS TEAM

A crisis team should be small, empowered, and cross-functional. It should include the following:

- Senior communications leadership
- Executive decision-makers
- Legal counsel
- Operational experts
- HR or people leadership
- A coordinator who manages information flow
- A digital intelligence lead

Everyone must know who speaks, who decides, and who activates partners.

AN IMMEDIATE PLACEHOLDER MESSAGE

A brief statement stabilizes early speculation: "We are aware of the situation and assessing the facts. We will provide more information shortly." This approach signals responsibility and presence.

MESSAGE ARCHITECTURE BASED ON THE FIVE C'S

Effective crisis communication rests on five principles:

- Clarity: say what you mean
- Conviction: communicate with direction
- Compassion: center people
- Consistency: align messages across channels
- Credibility: support statements with action

Steadiness matters more than perfection.

STAKEHOLDER SEQUENCING

Your most important audiences should hear from you first:

- Employees
- Regulators and partners
- Customers and communities
- Media
- Social audiences

Internal clarity reduces external confusion.

REAL-TIME INTELLIGENCE MONITORING

Crises evolve minute by minute. Leaders must watch:

- Social sentiment
- Misinformation trends
- Media framing
- Stakeholder reactions
- Narrative shifts

You cannot shape a narrative if you do not understand it.

MESSAGE DISCIPLINE ACROSS CHANNELS

Alignment prevents escalation. That means:

- Staying factual
- Avoiding emotional tone
- Correcting mistakes with transparency
- Moving sensitive conversations offline
- Avoiding public arguments
- Maintaining a human-centered tone

In a digital environment, discipline is survival.

Leadership Through a Crisis

Humans are emotional creatures. In a crisis, people react emotionally before they begin thinking rationally. People process threat, uncertainty, and concern long before they process logic. Because of this, leaders must manage both the situation and the emotional climate surrounding it.

The difference between crisis management and crisis leadership is simple. Crisis management is the set of actions that address the immediate issue. Crisis leadership is the behavior that guides people through uncertainty. It involves judgment, empathy, fairness, and the ability to reduce emotional noise.

Leaders should always ask themselves two questions. First, what is the fairest choice? Second, how will people experience that choice? Fairness is an underrated leadership tool. People do not always need to agree with your decision, but they need to feel that the decision is fair and that it was made with care.

Crisis leadership also requires clear communication. People will be judging your response. Your reputation will hang in the balance. In moments of pressure, character becomes visible, and your values become either real or exposed as performative.

Accountability is essential. Own the situation. Own the choices. Own the impact. When you communicate with empathy and fairness, people follow you more easily through difficult periods.

The Power of Community in Crisis

One of the most significant changes in crisis management is the central role of community. Crises now move through networks of people who talk, share, interpret, and spread information at speed. Your community can stabilize the narrative or fracture it.

Your community includes employees, partners, customers, investors, advocates, civic leaders, alumni, suppliers, neighbors, and industry peers. These groups can amplify your message or amplify misinformation. They can bring clarity or confusion. They can defend you or desert you.

To activate community support, leaders must:

- Communicate early
- Communicate honestly
- Provide context
- Share facts people can repeat
- Reinforce values
- Acknowledge supporters

Community support is built long before a crisis and becomes essential during one.

Crisis as a Reputation Catalyst

Handled well, a crisis can strengthen reputation instead of weakening it. Crises reveal character. They draw attention. They force clarity. They create moments when people listen more closely than usual.

I often return to a comment Rahm Emanuel made during the

2008 financial crisis. He said, "You never want a serious crisis to go to waste because it is an opportunity to do things you could not do before."

He was not encouraging opportunism. He was explaining what pressure can reveal. Crises break routines. They allow overdue changes to move forward. They expose what needs repair. They open space for reform and renewal.

During a crisis, stakeholders will have questions: Does leadership understand the moment? Will they communicate openly? Will they act decisively? Will their response match their values? When leaders meet those expectations, a crisis becomes a catalyst. It strengthens identity. It accelerates evolution. It reinforces integrity. Many organizations emerge stronger after a crisis because the crisis forced honesty, action, and learning. Crisis does not define you. Your response does.

A Bit of Star Power Turns Crisis into Opportunity

Every crisis has a risk side and an opportunity side. A recent example made that clear when Astronomer, a niche data operations firm, found itself at the center of a viral scandal. A video from a Coldplay concert showed the company's CEO and chief people officer in a moment that raised immediate questions about conduct and judgment. The clip spread quickly, and for a few days, the only thing most people knew about Astronomer was the video that put the company in the spotlight for the wrong reasons.[1]

Instead of hiding from the attention, the company found a way to redirect it. After the CEO resigned and leadership addressed the issue internally, Astronomer released a short promotional video featuring Gwyneth Paltrow as a temporary spokesperson. Because she has long-standing ties to Coldplay, the choice carried a hint of humor without minimizing the seriousness of what led to the resignations. The video, produced by Ryan Reynolds's creative agency, used a familiar cultural face to answer the questions people were already asking and then guided the conversation toward what the company actually does. The tone was light, but the strategy was serious. It shifted the focus from scandal to product, and it did so in a way that signaled confidence rather than defensiveness.

The reason the approach worked is simple. The company took responsibility first. It made a leadership change, affirmed its standards, and communicated its expectations for conduct. Only then did it use humor to engage the public and reclaim the narrative. The Paltrow video did not erase the original problem, but it reframed the moment and helped people understand the company beyond the viral clip. It also reminded audiences that a personal lapse by one leader does not always reflect the integrity of an entire organization.

The Astronomer case shows how an unexpected disruption can become a reputational reset when handled with clarity and balance. The company did not choose the moment that put it in front of millions of people, but it chose how to respond once the attention arrived. It acknowledged the issue, addressed it directly, and used creativity to steer the story toward its values and its work. A crisis that could have overshadowed the brand instead became an example of how tone, timing, and humility can turn an unwelcome spotlight into a chance to strengthen identity.

Crisis Resilience: Repair, Rebuild, Reinforce

After the immediate crisis passes, many organizations fall silent. They assume quiet reduces scrutiny. In reality, it often invites suspicion.

Resilience requires visible follow-through:

1. *Demonstrate repairs.* Show what is being improved or reformed. People want evidence.
2. *Reinforce your values.* Values matter most after the spotlight fades. Reaffirm them clearly.
3. *Reengage stakeholders.* Employees, partners, and customers need acknowledgment and updates.
4. *Conduct a learning review.* Evaluate what worked, what slowed you, and what must change.
5. *Adapt for the future.* Use lessons to strengthen systems and leadership capability.

Resilience is not about returning to normal. It is about emerging stronger, clearer, and more aligned.

AI in Crisis Management

Today's crises move faster than human monitoring alone can manage. AI-supported intelligence now plays an essential role in identifying early warning signs and shaping response strategies.

AI can enhance crisis work in several ways:

- Sentiment tracking
- Misinformation detection
- Narrative mapping
- Forecast modeling
- Network analysis
- Real-time stakeholder insight

AI does not replace leadership judgment. It sharpens it. It shortens the distance between signal and response. And in a world where misinformation can spread globally in minutes, this capability has become foundational.

Deepfakes and Synthetic Media: The New Crisis Trigger

The next era of crisis work will be shaped by synthetic media. Deepfakes, audio clones, and manipulated video are already active forces. They move quickly through networks and create confusion before leaders understand what has been circulated. Synthetic content can look convincing, but the deeper risk lies in how people react. Individuals respond emotionally to content long before they question its authenticity. In a crisis environment already defined by speed and uncertainty, synthetic media accelerates both.

Leaders must now plan for crises that begin with false or distorted material. A manufactured audio clip that sounds like a senior executive, a fabricated video involving an employee, or a synthetic image tied to a brand can trigger public reaction before an organization has a chance to confirm facts. This is why awareness and preparedness matter. You cannot wait until synthetic content spreads to decide how your organization will verify, respond, and communicate.

The leadership test in these moments is similar to that in any crisis, yet more compressed. Clarity, transparency, and speed become even more important. Stakeholders need to hear directly from you, in steady, human language that explains what is known, what is unknown, and what is being validated. People forgive uncertainty when leaders show presence and consistency. They do not forgive silence.

Synthetic media can also reinforce the importance of community. When people understand your values and believe your organization has a history of acting with integrity, it becomes harder for false narratives to take hold. Communities help correct misinformation, challenge fabricated material, and stabilize the public conversation. This makes the reputational work you do in calm periods essential. When synthetic content appears, you will rely on the relationships, credibility, and goodwill you have built. The organizations that weather these episodes most effectively are the ones that earned trust long before the crisis arrived.

Reputation in a Crisis-Defined World

We live in a time when crises arrive quickly, evolve unpredictably, and intersect with cultural forces that challenge leaders in new ways. Success now depends on a reputation-first mindset.

Reputation leadership means:

- Expecting crises
- Preparing during calm periods
- Acting with clarity and speed
- Communicating with honesty
- Treating values as operational commitments
- Engaging communities meaningfully
- Learning publicly and improving visibly

Crisis leadership today involves much more than merely limiting or minimizing damage. It requires demonstrating identity with consistency and courage. When you lead with values and clarity, you do more than survive the crisis. You strengthen the reputation that carries your organization forward.

TAKEAWAYS

- *Prepare before you need to.* Map vulnerabilities, define roles, and build crisis readiness into your culture.
- *Let your values lead under pressure.* Your reputation pillars must shape every decision and message.

- *Move quickly, but don't rush.* A fast, credible placeholder statement stabilizes early narratives.
- *Communicate to your stakeholders first.* Internal clarity reduces external chaos and strengthens community support.
- *Monitor in real time.* Crisis conversations shift by the minute; stay ahead of them.
- *Reinforce your identity after the storm.* Visible follow-through rebuilds trust and strengthens long-term reputation.

Chapter 7

IS YOUR MODERN BUSINESS RUNNING ON AN OLD REPUTATION MODEL?

In the traditional journey, reputation was shaped mainly through structured, top-down messaging and slower-moving information flows. Here's a breakdown of the basic steps of the traditional journey in the pre-digital era.

1. *Message creation (controlled communications).* Reputation started with carefully crafted messaging—press releases, advertising campaigns, corporate brochures, and speeches. These messages were designed by PR teams or agencies and approved by senior leadership.
2. *Media amplification (gatekeeper model).* Mainstream media (TV, newspapers, radio) acted as the primary amplifiers. Journalists and editors decided what got covered, shaping

public perception. Access to media was limited, giving brands greater control over what was seen and heard.

3. *Audience reception (perceived image).* Public audiences received the message passively. Trust and reputation were influenced by brand image, endorsements, and media portrayals—often with delayed feedback.

4. *Brand loyalty or dissatisfaction (lagging indicators).* Customer experiences—good or bad—took time to surface. Word of mouth existed, but it traveled slowly. Surveys, focus groups, and sales data were the main ways companies assessed reputation.

Today's journey is omnichannel and omnipresent. It essentially plays out in real time. It's emotionally driven and fueled by audience interaction. And because it's tied directly to business outcomes such as revenue and profit, it cannot be ignored or downplayed. Here are the hallmarks of the transition from the old journey to the new journey (see Table 7.1):

- Messaging has been replaced by *social signal interpretation.*

- Media gatekeepers have given way to *peer networks and influencers.*

- Brand image is shaped initially by promises, but *positive experiences must follow the promises.*

- Reputation is dynamic—*earned in moments, lost in seconds.*

TABLE 7.1: OLD VERSUS NEW REPUTATION JOURNEY

Stage	Traditional journey	Modern journey
1. Messaging	Controlled communications via press releases, brochures, ad campaigns. ***Key trait:*** *one-way, top-down communication*	Traditional messaging concepts and techniques are still used, but word of mouth and social media are much more powerful and persuasive. ***Key trait:*** *messaging is two-way, omnichannel, and omnipresent*
2. Amplification	Outreach to media gatekeepers, journalists, editors. ***Key trait:*** *reputation messaging flowed through gatekeepers*	Users and influencers share experiences through self-created or cocreated content on social media (TikTok, Reddit, YouTube). A large part of our job today is influencing the influencers! ***Key trait:*** *audiences amplify the brand message*
3. Audience engagement	Audiences receive messages passively; perceptions form slowly. ***Key trait:*** *linear and delayed feedback loop*	Audiences interact fluidly as promoters, critics, and observers. ***Key trait:*** *audiences are partners and cocreators, not receptacles*
4. Feedback/ outcome	Reputation is assessed via surveys, focus groups, and sales trends. ***Key trait:*** *feedback was lagging and episodic*	Reputation emerges in real time, driving relationship dynamics that lead to gains or losses in revenue and profit. ***Key trait:*** *reputation tied directly to business outcomes and revenue/profit growth*

The reputation journey clearly is alive and well; it's just a lot different than it was in the past. We can't predict exactly what the journey will look like in the future, but when you factor in the likely impacts of rapidly advancing technologies like generative AI and quantum computing, it's a sure bet that reputation will continue evolving. In the next chapter, we examine the evolutionary roots of reputation and see how it's inextricably woven into human culture.

TAKEAWAYS

- *Compare* your current reputation practices against modern benchmarks.
- *Identify* outdated tactics still in use and phase them out.
- *Highlight* quick wins to prove the value of agile, participatory approaches.
- *Educate* leadership on why control has shifted to communities and algorithms.
- *Build* culture that rewards adaptability, not rigid adherence to old models.

Part II

REPUTATION LEADERSHIP

Chapter 8

LEAD IT OR LOSE IT: REPUTATION STARTS AT THE TOP

Reputation requires constant attention, focus, and discipline. But most of all, reputation requires leadership. Everyone in an organization contributes to reputation, but the tone is always set at the top. When there's a gap between what the CEO says and what the CEO does, people notice. How leaders respond to events—especially in crisis—can have a lasting impact. Seasoned executives don't shy away from speaking the truth. In the long run, authenticity is still the best policy.

CEOs in the Reputation Hall of Fame

I've worked with some of the best CEOs in the world. They hunt for the truth and lead with it. They know honesty is one of the qualities people look for when they judge reputation. This instinct is hardwired into us.

What do leaders like Jensen Huang, Satya Nadella, Tim Cook, and Warren Buffett have in common? Beyond their obvious success, they all understand the indispensable value of reputation. Each embodies a strong personal brand and has imbued their company with reputability. Their products and services may be expected to perform, but it's their leadership reputations that inspire unusual confidence. If there were a "Reputation Hall of Fame" for CEOs, they'd be in it. A short list of legendary inductees would include the following.

STEVE JOBS, APPLE

When Jobs returned to Apple in 1997, the company was near bankruptcy, with its market share shrinking and product lineup struggling. With relentless focus and bold product launches—the iMac, iPod, iPhone, iPad—he repositioned Apple as a premium design brand for consumers willing to pay more for quality. Jobs's marketing genius and ability to frame Apple as the choice of design-conscious buyers restored trust in the company. Under his leadership, Apple's market capitalization soared. Today, it exceeds $3.5 trillion. Jobs's reputation for vision and creativity reshaped Apple—and the global tech landscape.

JAMES BURKE, JOHNSON & JOHNSON

Burke is the hero of the 1982 Tylenol crisis. After cyanide-laced capsules caused deaths, he immediately recalled 31 million bottles, introduced tamper-proof packaging, and launched a consumer safety campaign. His decisive response became a case study in crisis management and restored trust in both the brand and the company. The crisis also earned him a reputation that CEOs in healthcare and pharmaceuticals still strive to match today.

Don't Wait Until You're CEO

You don't need to sit in the corner office to elevate a company's reputation. Victoria Bunyard, a former CTO of IBM Northern Europe, championed the Mayflower Autonomous Ship project, showcasing IBM's AI capabilities and its commitment to sustainability. Her technical leadership and visible advocacy strengthened IBM's innovative image at a time when critics claimed the company was falling behind in AI. The timing of her contribution was crucial, proving that IBM still had the capacity to innovate and push boundaries in unexpected directions.

Superlative leaders share a willingness to lead publicly. They take credit for success and accept blame for failure. Many value privacy, but none are invisible. Jeff Bezos is an example: Even after stepping down as CEO, Bezos remains inseparable from Amazon in the public imagination.

In today's world, CEOs are no longer anonymous figures in gray flannel suits. They are high-profile influencers. And the correlation between a leader's reputation and the reputation of their organization has never been stronger.

TAKEAWAYS

- *Model* alignment between your words and actions—credibility begins with leaders.
- *Lead* publicly during crises; visible authenticity outlasts scripted statements.
- *Recognize* that your personal reputation is inseparable from your company's.
- *Develop* emerging leaders who champion reputation at every level.
- *Accept* that today's CEO is an influencer—every action, online or offline, is subject to real-time scrutiny.

Chapter 9

THE CEO'S OPERATING SYSTEM: REPUTATION BY DESIGN, NOT DEFAULT

Every organization tells the world who it is—not through slogans, but through the way it operates. Reputation, at its core, is the sum of those operations made visible. It's the reflection of thousands of choices made every day: how leaders act when no one is watching, how employees treat one another, how partners are selected, how the company responds when things go wrong.

We often speak of reputation as a halo that hovers above the business, something curated by communications or polished by marketing. In reality, reputation lives in the machinery of the enterprise—in hiring practices and pay equity, in supply chain ethics and customer service scripts, and in how finance reports results and how technology protects data. It is both mirror and engine, reflecting performance while driving it forward.

To operationalize reputation is to make that mirror intentional. It is the process of turning belief into behavior and behavior into measurable advantage. Every organizational function becomes a stakeholder in the reputational strategy. When each department understands its reputational impact, the organization begins to operate as one organism. It becomes responsive, coherent, and credible.

This integration has tangible results. Decision-making accelerates because friction is reduced. Innovation expands because people are allowed to fail intelligently. Culture becomes self-correcting because integrity is built into the workflow. What once required enforcement begins to happen naturally, reinforced by example and expectation rather than rules.

In the era of generative AI and instantaneous transparency, this coherence is no longer optional. Stakeholders judge companies less by what they say and more by how consistently they act. They study patterns, not press releases. They connect dots across platforms and markets to see whether an organization's story holds up under scrutiny. That scrutiny carries real weight: Research shows that 70 percent to 80 percent of a company's market value now comes from hard-to-assess intangible assets such as brand equity, intellectual capital, and goodwill.[1]

Operationalizing reputation is therefore not another program to manage; it is a different way to run the business. It asks every leader to view reputation not as a shield against criticism but as an internal operating principle. When credibility becomes embedded in every process—from strategy to service, from design to delivery—reputation stops being a by-product. It becomes the business model itself.

The journey of operationalizing reputation starts where all organizational energy originates—in the choices, tone, and behavior of leadership. That's where belief first becomes practice.

Executive Leadership

Reputation begins with leadership. The tone, transparency, and consistency of those at the top determine whether the organization inspires belief or invites skepticism. Every public statement, internal decision, or private gesture from leadership signals what the company stands for and whether it has earned credibility.

In an age of AI, deepfakes, and radical transparency, leaders cannot rely on silence as a shield. Absence leaves a vacuum that others will fill. Active visibility, through authentic communication, clear principles, and thoughtful engagement, builds a protective moat around both the leader and the enterprise.

When leaders demonstrate alignment between words and actions, their reputations become strategic assets. A strong leader's credibility cascades through the organization, amplifying culture, accelerating compliance, and enabling innovation. Conversely, reputational weakness at the top fractures culture, erodes credibility, and magnifies risk.

Leadership reputation is therefore not personal vanity. It is operational currency—the collateral on which every major decision depends. Leaders operationalize reputation through consistent behavior, transparent decisions, and follow-through that proves what they stand for.

Communications and Marketing

Communications is the transmission system of reputation. Every message that leaves the organization shapes how stakeholders perceive its integrity. But the effectiveness of the message depends on whether the organization's actions match the signals it's sending.

When an organization's reputation is high, its communications enhance credibility. But when reputation is low, even accurate information sounds defensive. Marketing and communications teams must therefore ensure that their messages align with reality. Overpromising destroys faster than underperformance. As the old saying reminds us, nothing kills a bad product faster than good advertising.

Operationalizing reputation in communications means designing a consistent "expectation architecture." Each message must be truthful, audience-aware, and synchronized with what the organization can deliver. The best communicators are translators of culture: They ensure that the promises made to the market align with the capabilities of the enterprise.

Modern AI tools allow for precise testing of tone, message, and audience response. Yet even the most sophisticated technologies are only parts of an overall process. Reputation still depends on authenticity—on showing, not spinning. Communications teams that understand this balance between narrative and proof occupy a pivotal role: They are both storytellers and stewards of credibility.

Sales and Business Development

Reputation enters the room before you do. It determines whether the conversation begins with curiosity or suspicion. In business development, reputation reduces friction, speeds negotiation, and expands opportunity.

A good reputation signals reliability and shared values, allowing partners to engage more deeply and more quickly. In a world where relationships often outweigh contracts, reputation can be the deciding factor in closing deals or forming alliances.

The buying landscape has shifted from *what and how* to *who and why*. Prospects now assess the moral identity of the organization: Who are these people, and why do they do what they do? Authenticity, empathy, and purpose are as influential as pricing or features.

Sales teams are also the organization's sensory network. They hear how reputation performs in the wild—what customers believe, doubt, or repeat. Feeding that intelligence back into leadership and marketing closes the loop between perception and reality.

When sales acts as both advocate and diagnostician, reputation becomes a living asset, continuously tested and refined in real time.

Customer Experience and Customer Success

Customer experience is where reputation earns its proof. Every interaction validates or contradicts the brand's promise.

A company with a strong reputation enjoys a longer forgiveness curve. When something goes wrong, a strong reputation earns the benefit of the doubt because history suggests fairness and competence. Conversely, when a brand's reputation is weak, small failures feel like betrayals.

Operationalizing reputation at the customer interface requires empathy, responsiveness, and a commitment to follow-through. Service teams should be trained to resolve issues *and* to safeguard the organization's reputation.

Customers do not expect flawless performance; they expect honesty and care. A company that turns mistakes into moments of integrity strengthens its reputation. Each recovery handled well reinforces the idea that this is an organization worthy of loyalty.

Ultimately, customer success is not an afterthought. It is the ongoing referendum on whether reputation lives up to its billing.

Human Resources, People, and Culture

Reputation is the magnetic field that either draws talent or repels it. People want to work for organizations that reflect their values, respect their individuality, and deliver on their promises.

A respected company culture does more than attract talent; it retains and inspires it. Employees who feel proud of where they work become informal ambassadors. They carry the company's story into every meeting, post, and interaction.

Reputation now ranks among the top factors in talent decisions, especially for younger employees who choose employers based on values as much as opportunity. This is why operationalizing reputation through HR begins with alignment: The external brand must match the internal reality. If candidates are sold a vision of creativity but encounter bureaucracy, the disconnect spreads through networks instantly.

HR professionals also safeguard the organization's internal reputation. Policies, leadership development, and employee communication should reinforce openness and transparency. Culture is not built by slogans; it is built by consistent experience.

In the end, HR doesn't just manage people; it manages belief. A company's internal reputation shapes its external one. When employees feel confident and respected, that confidence and respect radiate outward.

Operations and Supply Chain

Supply chain is where reputation becomes real. The integrity of materials, labor practices, and sustainability commitments is reflected in every product and service an organization delivers. A single lapse (such as a mislabeled ingredient, a failed audit, or a video from a supplier facility) can ignite scrutiny that outweighs years of positive messaging.

More than half of major reputation crises in the past decade trace back to supply chain failures, whether they be safety issues, sourcing breakdowns, labor conditions, or environmental impact. This makes supply chain not a backstage function but a reputational front line where operational discipline becomes public proof.

Operationalizing reputation here requires visibility: the ability to know how vendors behave, how materials are sourced, and how risks move through the system. Strong supply chains reinforce reputation through consistency. Weak ones magnify exposure.

Pressure on costs often collides with expectations for ethics and sustainability. The organizations that navigate this tension well institutionalize standards, monitor performance, and treat supplier partnerships as extensions of their own credibility. When disruptions occur, as they inevitably do, responsiveness becomes the true reputational test. Clarity, speed, and accountability signal that the organization takes its commitments seriously.

Finance and Investor Relations

In finance, reputation converts directly to valuation. The perceived integrity of leadership and the credibility of disclosures influence capital access, cost of funds, and investor confidence.

Investors bet on character as much as cash flow. A company with an excellent reputation can raise capital faster, negotiate better terms, and weather downturns with less volatility. Conversely, even profitable firms struggle when markets doubt their honesty or competence.

Reputation is also a buffer against bad news. Companies with a track record of transparency earn forgiveness when results falter. Investors grant latitude because they believe the organization will recover with integrity.

Operationalizing reputation in finance means ensuring that truth is consistent across all reporting, from quarterly statements to informal briefings. Integrity is not a communications issue; it is a line item in enterprise value.

In the capital markets, credibility is currency—and reputation is the mint that prints it.

Product Innovation and R&D

Reputation fuels permission to innovate. Stakeholders tolerate experimentation, and even failure, when they have confidence in the organization's motives and competence.

Innovation thrives in cultures that encourage calculated risk-taking. When leadership treats failure as learning, teams push boundaries with confidence. This "risk permission" is reputational capital at work.

A reputation for innovation also attracts talent and partners. Brilliant minds want to contribute to brands known for creativity and courage. The company's track record signals whether new ideas will be nurtured or stifled.

Operationalizing reputation in R&D means aligning product development with brand values. Privacy, security, and ethical design must be embedded from concept to launch. Each new product or feature should not only meet functional needs but also reinforce the organization's integrity. When innovation and reputation move in sync, progress is self-sustaining.

Legal, Regulatory, and Compliance

Reputation and compliance are inseparable. A company known for integrity faces less scrutiny and greater goodwill from regulators, partners, and juries.

Legal teams play a dual role in operationalizing reputation: They protect the enterprise from external risk and ensure internal adherence to values. Ethical consistency in how laws are interpreted and applied defines the organization's moral fabric.

In litigation or crisis, reputation becomes an invisible advocate. Regulators and courts treat reputable actors differently from habitual offenders. The perceived fairness of a company's behavior often shapes the outcomes it receives.

Legal compliance is not a box to check; it's a public signal of self-governance. Every policy, contract, and disclosure tells the world what kind of organization this is.

Technology, IT, and Cybersecurity

Technology is now the front line of reputational risk. Data breaches, privacy violations, and AI misuse can destroy years of credibility overnight.

Operationalizing reputation in technology means embedding transparency into digital design. When a crisis occurs, honesty and speed of disclosure define recovery. Companies that communicate clearly about what happened, why, and how they'll fix it often emerge stronger.

Partnerships also signal integrity. Certifications and collaborations with trusted technology providers build confidence among customers and investors. The company you keep, whether in the cloud, in your data stack, or in your security ecosystem, reflects your values.

Reputation in IT is about safety, integrity, and foresight. Stakeholders assume that what's secure is also ethical. Protecting data and respecting privacy are no longer technical obligations; they are moral ones.

In the digital era, reputation is infrastructure. Technology doesn't just enable operations; it enables belief.

ESG and Corporate Responsibility

Environmental, social, and governance (ESG) performance is no longer a communications exercise; it is a reputational baseline. Stakeholders expect organizations to act responsibly, measure impact, and disclose progress.

Operationalizing reputation through ESG means integrating ethics into everyday operations and strategy. Sustainability, inclusion, and community investment must connect directly to business objectives.

Reputation in this domain depends on transparency. Overstated claims or selective disclosures are punished swiftly. Authenticity comes from measurable action: reduced emissions, equitable hiring, accountable governance.

A strong ESG reputation attracts investors, customers, and employees who want to align with purposeful enterprises. It also builds resilience, because companies acting responsibly earn the benefit of the doubt when challenges arise. Corporate responsibility, when appropriately executed and performed consistently, is character at scale.

Board and Governance

Governance is the conscience of reputation. Boards translate principles into oversight, ensuring that ethics, strategy, and accountability stay aligned.

A reputable board balances innovation with integrity. It asks hard questions, anticipates risk, and safeguards long-term credibility. Governance failures, by contrast, are always reputational—signaling negligence, complacency, or self-interest.

Operationalizing reputation at the board level means embedding it into decision frameworks: succession planning, executive compensation, risk tolerance, and disclosure policy. Reputation should be treated not as a soft factor but as a measurable component of enterprise value. Organizations that integrate reputation into planning cycles can make decisions faster and with greater clarity about long-term impact.

A credible board models transparency and fairness. Its behavior sets the standard for the entire organization. When governance works, reputation flows upward as much as downward; it reinforces the belief that leadership can be trusted with both power and purpose.

Sourcing and Manufacturing

Every product carries a moral footprint. The conditions under which it is made—materials, labor, sustainability—now shape consumer and investor perception as much as design or price.

Operationalizing reputation in manufacturing means treating suppliers as partners in ethics. Traceability, auditability, and continuous improvement become nonnegotiable.

A company's supply chain is its shadow reputation: unseen by most but decisive in crisis. Transparency about sourcing, production standards, and worker welfare builds confidence among stakeholders.

When the manufacturing backbone is ethical and resilient, the brand stands on solid ground. When it isn't, no amount of storytelling can compensate. Reputation, once again, is what remains when the lights go out.

A Shared Responsibility

Reputation becomes operational only when it is shared across the organization. Each department should understand its role in earning and protecting reputation. It is not the job of communications or leadership alone; reputation is the collective behavior of the enterprise.

Every function is a lens through which stakeholders perceive integrity. Together, they create a self-reinforcing loop: Leadership shapes culture; culture drives performance; performance shapes reputation; reputation, in turn, strengthens leadership.

This is the new architecture of credibility—decentralized, transparent, and systemic. When reputation is embedded in the operations of every function, it ceases to be a narrative and becomes a fact.

• • •

When reputation becomes operational, it becomes durable and sustainable. It stops depending on personalities or moments and starts drawing its strength from the systems that shape everyday behavior.

Studies also show that companies with strong reputations rebound from crises far faster than competitors with weaker reputational footing. That resilience is not an accident. It is the result of clarity in values, consistency in decisions, and alignment between what a company says and what it proves. When every department understands its role in that alignment, reputation shifts from a communications outcome to a competitive advantage. It becomes a source of stability in uncertainty and a force that accelerates performance in moments that matter.

TAKEAWAYS

- *Reputation is systemic.* It flows through every function, not just marketing or communications.
- *Credibility compounds through proof.* Alignment between words and actions builds reputation.
- *Operational readiness equals reputational strength.* Promises must match capacity.
- *Transparency beats perfection.* How an organization responds under pressure reinforces its existing reputation, creates new beliefs (positive or negative), or changes nothing.

- *Governance is the conscience of reputation.* Oversight and ethics determine durability.
- *Reputation is leadership in motion.* Every department expresses it; every decision tests it.

Chapter 10

MANAGING REPUTATION IN THE SCROLL AGE

In today's world, reputations rise and fall at the speed of a tweet or a trending hashtag. I've seen it firsthand, over and over again: Organizations watch as their public standing crashes overnight. What used to be a slow burn is now a flash fire. That's the reality we're dealing with: Reputational change has become faster, more personal, and more unforgiving than ever. If we're going to succeed, we need to stop trying to slow things down and instead build the capacity to keep up.

We're not going to slow down the information cycle. That's the first thing I tell clients. What we can do, however, is get smarter and faster in how we listen, how we respond, and how we manage reputation in real time. That starts with data. Yet too many organizations make decisions based on limited streams of insight from disparate or disconnected information silos. When you're responsible for managing reputation, you should be looking at a variety of inputs, such as call center feedback, media mentions, social listening, influencer engagement metrics, employee sentiment surveys, product return data, app store reviews, customer journey analytics, and internal whistleblower reports.

But the hard part is integrating all these streams and developing a genuinely holistic reputation strategy. Ideally, everyone in the organization should be reading from the same sheet of music. Do your client representatives and department leaders share the same facts about the company's products and services? Are managers and executives truly aware of the many touchpoints where the company engages with customers?

It's not enough to polish up dashboards for the next board meeting. We need to democratize data across the organization. Let it speak. Let it tell us things we didn't expect to hear. The problem isn't access; it's mindset. Far too many reputation decisions are still being made on gut instinct, while clear, powerful, and real-time data is sitting in the background, underutilized.

Learn from Political Campaigns

I've worked with people who run national political campaigns, and I can tell you this: Nothing is more sophisticated when it comes to understanding public opinion and shaping behavior block by block. In politics, we use data to win counties, towns, neighborhoods. Why not apply that same thinking to brands?

Here's an example. One of our clients is a large retailer. They've been hit hard by public perception issues tied to DEI commitments and subsequent retractions. The old playbook would say to run a national campaign and hope the message trickles down.

But that's not working. What we're exploring now is a localized strategy—identifying the twelve or so key states where the retailer has the most stores and building tailored messaging for each one. This is reputation management at the ground level. It's bold, yes. It's different. But it's what the moment demands.

I say that not to be dramatic but to be accurate. The way people consume information is highly individualized. We build our own news feeds. We follow who we choose. Mass messaging simply doesn't work the way it once did. To influence perception now, we have to get local, get granular.

And yes, that means playing offense and defense at the same time. We need to "boost and blunt": Elevate the positive narrative while softening the impact of the negative. We need to build reputational durability, a kind of Teflon layer that can withstand inevitable gaffes and missteps. If you've done the work to earn trust on the ground, people are more likely to give you the benefit of the doubt when the unexpected happens.

The good news? We have the tools. We can mine, curate, and deploy messaging in real time. The challenge isn't technological; it's cultural. In marketing, this level of precision is standard; brands can guide you to a specific aisle in CVS. But in corporate communications, we're still relying on legacy approaches. That has to change. It means reshaping your message continuously, not waiting for the next quarter; responding to comments and direct engagements within twenty-four hours; being authentic, timely, and trend-aware, all while staying true to a central goal.

That's what I mean when I talk about "laddering up." Your tactics and messages might change week to week, but they're always in service of core reputational goals: restoring confidence, driving traffic, fueling business growth, and attracting talent. To be clear, this isn't just a response mechanism. It's proactive. It's deliberate. And it's essential. If we want to protect and rebuild reputation, we need to engage with the public the way they're engaging with us: personally, locally, and frequently.

One of the most profound changes I've witnessed in my career is the democratization of storytelling. We used to say, "the victor writes the history." But today, that's no longer true. Everyone writes the story. Everyone has a platform. The narrative process is networked, shared, and collaborative.

That's what excites me. We're living in a moment where we don't just manage reputation; we cocreate it with the public. That's powerful. That's personal. If we embrace that reality, we can build reputations that not only survive disruption but thrive in it.

Your Smartphone Is Eating Your Mind

If you're looking for a reason why the job of reputation management has become so excruciatingly difficult over the past dozen or so years, look no further than your smartphone.

I knew the world around me had really changed when I began sleeping with my smartphone. No, it's not what you think. Let's just say that my smartphone used to spend its nights on the desk in my home office. Now I bring it into our bedroom every night, where it rests on a small table near my pillow, never far from reach.

Nowadays we all use our smartphones all the time and everywhere. We are all fellow addicts, captives to our smartphones and enthralled by many of their adjacent technologies. Who knew that the basic premise of the movie *Her* would become our common reality so quickly? Science fiction doesn't stay fiction for very long these days.

Short attention spans are the new normal and we need to understand why. It's not because all of us have suddenly become idiots—it's because we have too much stimuli competing for our limited attention!

The influencers whose livelihoods depend on grabbing and holding our attention understand this. They know their windows of opportunity are momentary. So they act quickly. Very quickly! Once upon a time, reputation was measured over decades; now it can vary wildly within days or even minutes. Reputation has become a volatile substance, ready to explode without warning.

Both the speed and the magnitude of reputational change have increased dramatically. Not only can your reputation rise or fall faster than ever before, but the highs have become higher and the lows have become lower!

An example of this phenomenon is occurring in real time. As I write these words, Tesla stock is rebounding after a two-month decline. Despite the rebound, Tesla shares are still trading roughly 41 percent lower than they were in December 2024.[1] Tesla's volatility isn't directly related to the quality of the cars it manufactures. Instead, it's largely the result of Elon Musk's reputation at the present moment. I can't predict the future price of Tesla stock, but I can say with reasonable certainty that Tesla shareholders are in for a rough ride. I'm not the only person who feels this way; several Wall Street analysts have called for Musk to either stop talking politics or step down.[2]

When the CEO of a company is a celebrity, his or her reputation can have a direct and immediate impact on the company's value. I doubt that future historians will remember Musk in the same glowing terms as Steve Jobs and Warren Buffett. But will he be lumped in with bad apples like Jeffrey Skilling (Enron), Dennis Kozlowski (Tyco International), Elizabeth Holmes (Theranos), and Sam Bankman-Fried (FTX), who not only brought themselves down but also brought down or severely damaged the companies they ran? Only time will tell. That said, I'm sure Tesla shareholders are hoping Musk's seesawing reputation doesn't become a fatal distraction.

TAKEAWAYS

- *Consolidate* data streams into a unified view of reputation risks and opportunities.
- *Train* teams to act on signals immediately, not after quarterly reviews.
- *Monitor* memes, hashtags, and micro-trends—any one of them can ignite into a reputational flashpoint.
- *Embed* reputation dashboards into daily leadership routines.
- *Shift* from passive monitoring to active reputation management in real time.

Chapter 11

REPUTATION IN TRANSLATION: SPEAK THEIR LANGUAGE, KEEP YOUR VOICE

One of the most underrated forms of creativity in reputation work is the ability to "read the room" and deliver your message in a relatable way. It's about adapting your voice and cultural references to connect with your audiences by knowing the "language world" you're stepping into and how to make your message resonate there.

In communication circles, this adaptive skill is sometimes called code-switching—the ability to adjust tone, language, and reference points depending on who you're speaking to. In reputation work, the stakes for getting this right are high. Misjudge the tone, and you can lose credibility even if your facts were correct.

Think of every audience you face as its own little language world. You might use one tone talking to employees on the plant floor, another when addressing investors, and yet a different cadence when trying to build a bridge with skeptical stakeholders. In this context, code-switching is all about nuance and empathy.

Stephen Adubato, a writer and philosophy professor based in New York, makes the case that code-switching lets you show people you speak their language, without necessarily agreeing with their frame. It's about understanding them, not pandering, and that builds real connection.[1]

Every demographic segment—political group, generation, region—has its idioms and triggers. Use the right metaphor, tone, or reference, and you create instant resonance. Miss the mark, and you sound robotic, tone-deaf, or worse: alien.

Code-switching, on the other hand, opens emotional doors. When you can speak someone else's language, they're much more likely to engage with you. Remember, the goal isn't speaking down or speaking up to an audience. The goal is speaking with the audience, having a genuine dialogue, an authentic conversation.

For example, IKEA's playful social media campaigns show how deep cultural attunement can spark engagement across very different audiences. From cheekily sliding into the DMs of late-night scrollers in Canada with tailored offers, to serving free chips to those who have suffered "chip theft" by local seagulls in Brighton, UK, to creatively tapping into the Japanese market with their use of their shark toy Blåhaj as the mascot that adds local charm. All these efforts helped IKEA grow their global audience. Each country has its own social media channels and often different local content that changes regularly.[2] These campaigns highlight how brands must tailor their creative approach—not just the message itself, but the cultural references and tone.

Handled well, this kind of adaptation is the opposite of being deceptive or "putting on an act." It's about empathy and awareness, recognizing that different audiences have different cultural cues, priorities, and comfort zones, all while speaking in ways that acknowledge those differences without abandoning your core identity. In an age of radical transparency, the ability to adjust while staying true to your brand is a subtle but powerful reputational advantage.

What makes this especially powerful is that code-switching is scalable. It applies whether you're crafting a Super Bowl ad or responding to a single customer on TikTok. Both moments matter, and both require the creativity to meet people where they are. Reputation isn't built only in press releases or carefully scripted campaigns; it's also shaped in the micro-moments where audiences feel seen, heard, and understood.

This is where creativity and discipline intersect. You can't improvise your way into credibility, but you also can't cling to one rigid voice in every situation. The art lies in flexing without breaking, adapting tone and expression while holding firmly to your core values. That balance is what separates brands that thrive from those that stumble.

Leaders should remember that every interaction is reputational theater. The words you choose, the analogies you use, even the timing of your response—all send cultural signals. Over time, those signals accumulate into a pattern that becomes your reputation. Creativity in this sense isn't decorative; it's structural. It's the force that allows your message to travel across different contexts, bridge divides, and maintain authenticity in an environment where skepticism runs high.

Handled this way, code-switching isn't just a communications tactic. It's a form of creative leadership, an everyday practice that builds trust, fosters engagement, and earns reputation capital that can't be bought any other way.

TAKEAWAYS

- *Practice* code-switching; adapt tone and style without compromising authenticity.
- *Train* teams to read cultural signals across diverse audiences.
- *Design* messages that flex contextually but stay anchored to core values.
- *Study* global examples like IKEA to understand cultural fluency in action.
- *Treat* adaptation as empathy—the hallmark of reputational strength.

Chapter 12

LEADERSHIP PERSPECTIVES

Leaders shape reputation long before a brand enters the world. They influence how the organization behaves, how decisions are made, and how people interpret what the company stands for. In earlier chapters, we explore the leadership principles that create stability in moments of change. Those ideas help explain why reputation is not an image. It is the lived experience people have when they work with or encounter an organization.

In the following pages, we share the perspectives of six leaders who have spent their careers navigating complexity. Each offers a different view of how reputation forms under pressure and how leaders strengthen it through consistent behavior. Some lead global brands. Some advise political figures. Some build systems that keep organizations aligned. All believe reputation starts inside the company, shaped by culture and leadership choices.

These conversations do not offer a single doctrine. They show how reputation develops in real environments with real constraints. They remind us that leadership is defined by behavior.

And they show that reputational strength grows when leaders communicate clearly, act with purpose, and take responsibility for the systems that support the work.

How Leadership Behavior Builds Reputational Strength

INTERVIEW WITH ANTON VINCENT, PRESIDENT OF MARS SNACKING NORTH AMERICA AND GLOBAL ICE CREAM AT MARS INC.

I invited Anton Vincent to contribute to this book because he leads with clarity and personal integrity at a scale that influences millions of households. His approach to leadership reflects something I believe deeply: Reputation begins in the room long before it reaches the world. Anton has a rare ability to shape culture through steady example.

His experience at Mars Wrigley shows how internal behavior becomes external perception. He understands that consistency, openness, and responsible decision-making create the conditions that allow brands to thrive. Anton's perspective offers a grounded look at how strong reputations are built from the inside out.

The first thing you notice about Anton Vincent is the calm. It is not passive calm. It is a grounded presence, the kind that comes from knowing who you are, knowing why you lead, and understanding what others need from you. In a business culture full of agitation and hurry, Anton brings a steadiness that feels rare.

He often talks about leadership as something lived in daily

behaviors rather than big moments. "People watch everything," he says, not as a warning but as a reminder. "Teams build their expectations by observing what leaders do when things are easy and when things are not. Consistency becomes a signal. It tells people whether they should move confidently or hold back."

For Anton, reputation begins long before anybody outside the organization forms an opinion. "If people feel clarity, they act with more energy. If they sense confusion, they slow down." He believes that the temperature inside a company is never separate from the one outside. "The external world eventually sees what the internal world feels," he says. "This is one of my simplest and strongest insights about leadership."

At Mars Wrigley, he uses the M&M's brand to explain accessible leadership. "M&M's have endured for decades because people see themselves in it—their events, the fun, and enjoyment. It is welcoming. And it meets people where they are: in groups, on their own, in business, and in everyday life." Anton believes leaders can learn from M&M's inclusiveness and openness. "When environments feel human and familiar, people take part more freely. When they feel rigid or closed, people retreat. Reputation grows from those accumulated emotional choices," he says.

He learned early in his career that leadership cannot be built on moments of performance. Organizations sense whether a leader's presence is real or theatrical. "People know when you're reaching for effect and when you're genuine," he says. "It is in how you respond to tension, how you explain a setback, how you make room for someone who has not spoken yet. These actions shape culture more powerfully than a slogan or a speech."

As a leader, Anton defines integrity as alignment between belief, behavior, and outcome. "Integrity isn't just a moral idea; it's an operational one," he says. "Integrity is a performance driver because it removes friction. People do not waste energy guessing what their leaders mean. They can see it."

Pressure reveals whether values are real. Anton believes, "When values shift to match circumstances, people lose confidence. But when leaders absorb pressure without losing themselves, the organization gains stability." He does not romanticize pressure. "Challenges are a part of leadership that must be handled with care so others can stay grounded," he observes.

Anton describes leadership as a responsibility contract. Not a contract written down, but one carried in behavior. "The responsibility includes ownership, generosity, fairness, and the willingness to be visible when something goes wrong. These qualities shape internal perception more than any external communication. People believe in leaders who share credit and accept responsibility. It is the pattern of these choices that builds a leader's reputation inside the company and eventually outside it."

Anton often talks about the "temperature" of an organization. "Warm cultures encourage participation. Cold cultures encourage silence," according to Anton. "Leaders set the temperature whether they intend to or not. A warm culture is not free of accountability. It is where people feel safe enough to contribute their best thinking because they know how their contributions will be received."

"Purpose," he says, "is the company's orientation point. It is not the same as ambition. Purpose explains why you are doing the work at all." When purpose is clear, teams interpret change with less anxiety. "Teams are not surprised by shifts in strategy when they recognize the principles that guide those shifts. Purpose gives movement meaning and becomes something others can sense, even from outside the company."

Anton's commitment to representation is equally pragmatic. Leadership, he believes, must resemble the world it serves. "Representation is not decoration. It influences decisions. It shapes how companies interpret consumer behavior and how they imagine their own future."

Consistency is a reputational asset, according to Anton. "In a noisy world, consistency communicates reliability. People lean toward leaders and brands that behave predictably in a good way. Consistency builds room for creativity because it provides a stable base." Chaos might inspire a burst of activity, but consistency builds things that last. "Calm is not the absence of action," he says. "It is the condition that allows action to matter."

In Anton's view, reputation becomes legacy. "Titles fade. Strategies get replaced. But the behaviors leaders normalize continue long after they are gone. If people still make grounded decisions when the leader is no longer in the room, then that leader built something real. Reputation is continuity."

His leadership story is not flashy. It is steady, human, and deeply attentive to how people feel when they walk into work each day. This is why his voice matters in any conversation about reputation. "Reputational strength does not come from campaigns or declarations," he reminds us. "It comes from culture. It comes from the daily behavior of leaders who understand that people are watching, not to judge, but to decide how they themselves will show up."

Anton leads with the understanding that reputation is built the same way trust once was. "Reputation is built behavior by behavior, choice by choice, day by day. Not through performance, but through the quiet consistency of how leaders carry themselves when nobody is looking."

Reputation Leadership: Resilient, Real, and Ready for What's Next

INTERVIEW WITH LESLIE MCGIBBON, CHIEF CORPORATE AFFAIRS AND BRAND OFFICER AT BT GROUP

Leslie McGibbon brings a rare blend of clarity and steadiness to his leadership at BT Group, the United Kingdom's leading fixed and mobile communications provider. His work across continents and industries has given him a deep understanding of how organizations earn their reputations from within. Leslie has led in environments where pressure is constant and expectations shift quickly, yet he continues to show how grounded behavior shapes the way people interpret a company's identity.

"I believe reputation grows strongest when behavior and identity match, and when leaders help people make sense of change with honesty and purpose," he emphasizes. "Resilient reputations are built one decision at a time inside the organization long before they reach the public."

Leslie McGibbon carries himself with the assurance of someone who has seen pressure from every angle. He has led communication and corporate affairs across industries that rarely give leaders the benefit of the doubt. He has lived inside global companies where every action lands on front pages or in parliament. Through it all, he developed a simple belief: "Organizations and individuals earn their reputations in the same way—how they behave in the moments that matter."

He does not speak like a theorist. He speaks like someone who has been in the room when decisions had consequences. "Leaders set the emotional temperature of a company not by what they say but by how they act," he observes. "People know when the inside is different from the outside, and the public eventually senses when a company's story does not match its behavior. Conversely, when behavior and identity line up, your reputation grows stronger almost automatically."

Leslie came to this understanding through years of working across cultures. "People everywhere respond to clarity," he says. "They do not expect perfection, but they do expect honesty. They also expect leaders to face reality rather than avoid it." In his view, resilience begins with the willingness to acknowledge what is true even when it is inconvenient.

He remembers moments when teams felt overwhelmed by shifting expectation. "Technology accelerated. Regulation expanded. Market conditions changed without warning. In these periods, people needed something steady to orient themselves. Leaders provide that orientation by giving meaning to the organization's actions and showing how the work connects to the future. People want to know what they are part of," he says. When that understanding is present, teams navigate uncertainty with less fear.

His philosophy of reputation leadership comes down to three attributes: "It's resilience, realism, and readiness that matter. The first is emotional. The second is intellectual. The third is operational."

Resilience means the organization can absorb pressure without losing itself. Leslie is quick to point out, "Resilience is not stoicism. It is the ability to stay grounded without becoming rigid. When people see leaders adapt with honesty and calm, they feel steadier themselves. A company cannot control the public conversation, but it can control the spirit with which it participates."

Realism, for Leslie, is the discipline of facing facts and understanding how audiences actually think. "Leaders often overestimate how much people care about the organization's point of view. This creates a gap between intent and perception," he believes. "Good reputation leaders reduce that gap by speaking plainly and listening without defensiveness. They do not pretend the world sees them as they wish to be seen. They work with the perception that exists and earn credibility through behavior."

Readiness is the ability to move with intention when change arrives. Leslie has led through crises where information was incomplete and the stakes were high. "Readiness grows from a culture that values clear roles, purposeful communication, and the right tempo of decision-making. People handle change better when they understand how decisions get made," he says. "Transparency becomes a reputational strength because it reduces uncertainty."

Leslie's leadership story is shaped by humility. He does not position himself as the hero. He positions the company as a collection of human beings who want to contribute and feel proud of their work. "Reputation is the shared outcome of thousands of decisions made by people who want to do the right thing, even when the right thing is hard," he says. "My role is to give those people a framework that helps them move with integrity and confidence."

His experience across industries ranging from electronics to pharmaceuticals to hospitality taught him that reputation breaks down when leaders try to perform rather than behave. "Audiences can sense when an organization is projecting an image instead of living an identity," he notes. "The solution is not better messaging, but better alignment. Leaders must model the values they expect others to uphold. Reputation starts with what the people inside the company believe about the company," he says. "If the inside belief is strong and grounded, the outside view eventually follows."

One of Leslie's greatest strengths is his ability to bring coherence to complexity. He understands that large organizations often struggle to express themselves clearly because they have too many internal voices competing for attention. "Leaders must help simplify the story," he says. "Not reduce it but clarify it. When a company knows how to explain itself to its own people, it becomes much easier to explain itself to the world."

He also believes representation matters. "Teams pay attention to who sits at the leadership table. They notice whether different perspectives are included and respected. Representation without influence is decoration. Representation with influence is credibility." Leslie has seen how the presence of diverse leaders improves decisions and strengthens the company's relationship with society.

What sets Leslie apart is his belief that reputation is not a communications project. "Reputation is a leadership act. It is not measured by volume or visibility. It is measured by whether people believe the organization behaves in ways that make sense and reflect its stated values. When leaders live those values, reputation becomes resilient because it is built on truth," he explains.

Leslie McGibbon's leadership philosophy is not complicated, but it is not easy. "It requires consistency, clarity, and the courage to face things as they are. It requires listening with humility and acting with purpose. It requires leaders who understand that reputation is shaped every day, in every room, by the choices people make and the culture those choices create," he states firmly.

This is why Leslie's perspective matters. He does not offer a formula. He offers a way of being. He is a leader who faces complexity with clarity and guides organizations toward a future where behavior and identity move in alignment. A future where reputation grows not from performance, but from the steady, honest work of people committed to being real, resilient, and ready for what comes next.

Reputation Is the Multiplier: The Leadership Currency That Speeds Belief

INTERVIEW WITH SIMON WHITEHEAD, CEO OF PORTLAND

I asked Simon Whitehead of Portland, a strategic communications consultancy specializing in public affairs, corporate affairs, and geopolitics, to talk about his career operating at the sharp edge of global communication and risk. Simon understands how speed, exposure, and cultural complexity shape the environment leaders navigate today and brings clear thinking to a world that often feels chaotic and accelerated.

Simon believes that "reputation can hold steady even when the context is not. Authenticity, preparation, and quality help leaders move with confidence in moments when others hesitate."

Simon moves through the world with an alert, centered awareness, as if he is always absorbing signals that others miss. "After years at the helm of a global consultancy, I've gained an instinct for the changing pressures that surround modern leadership. I see patterns and understand the environment leaders must navigate today, where information moves too fast, where emotion can outpace accuracy, and where perception becomes reality in an instant."

"The speed is real," he says. "People form judgments quickly, and leaders have to understand the currents before they step into them." He speaks not as a warning but as a practical observation. "Leaders cannot slow the environment. They can only strengthen themselves so the environment does not pull them off balance."

For Simon, reputation is the multiplier that allows leaders to move with confidence. "When an organization has a strong reputation, people grant it the benefit of the doubt. They believe the organization means well even when outcomes are imperfect. This belief speeds decisions and reduces friction. Without that reputational foundation, every move becomes harder and slower because people hesitate to follow."

He learned early on that leaders cannot wait for clarity before acting. "Clarity rarely arrives fully formed," in Simon's experience. "Leaders must interpret the moment, make decisions with imperfect information, and communicate those decisions in ways that feel grounded. Reputation gives them permission to do that. It is the currency that buys time, patience, and understanding."

Simon does not see reputation as something crafted in a conference room. He sees it as something earned through patterns. "People do not watch a leader once," he says. "They watch repeatedly. They look for evidence. They measure consistency. They test whether words match behavior. Over time, those patterns build a reservoir of belief that speeds everything else that follows."

Simon has sat with leaders who felt overwhelmed by the pace of global events. He has watched them face decisions involving geopolitics, public health, technology, and social expectation. "Leadership in these moments depends on preparation and presence. Preparation gives leaders a base of knowledge they can draw from. Presence gives them the ability to stay centered when the world demands quick action."

Simon learned that preparation without presence becomes rigidity. "Presence without preparation becomes improvisation," he says. "Leaders need both. When they have both, they can move with speed without losing their footing."

In his work with clients, he has seen how a well-managed reputation creates room for leaders to act boldly. "Reputation gives organizations the freedom to innovate, to explain, to take responsibility, and to move forward. This is the true value of reputation. It accelerates belief. It reduces doubt. It allows people inside the company to rally around decisions because they trust the judgment behind them, even when outcomes are not yet clear."

Simon also understands that modern audiences expect leaders to show humanity. "People interpret silence as indifference. They want leaders who communicate with honesty and humility. Not theatrical vulnerability, but real vulnerability. You do not have to have all the answers, but you do have to help people understand how you are thinking about the moment," he explains.

"Quality is a reputational anchor," he believes. "Leaders can move quickly without cutting corners if they build systems that support thoughtful decisions." He has seen organizations struggle because they equated speed with carelessness. Simon argues, "Speed is not the enemy of quality. Confusion is. When leaders communicate with clarity and intention, people sense the care behind the action."

He also believes diversity is essential to reputational strength. "Diversity isn't a slogan; it's a structural advantage," he says. "Diverse teams see risk earlier. They interpret signals differently. They challenge assumptions before those assumptions become blind spots. When leaders surround themselves with people who think differently, they increase their accuracy and reduce surprises."

Simon has a quiet confidence that comes from experience. He does not prescribe formulas. He offers patterns. He pays attention to how people respond under pressure. He watches how leaders communicate when stakes are high. He looks at momentum, not individual moments, because reputation grows in arcs, not snapshots.

"Leaders must take responsibility for the meaning people make of their actions," he says. "Even when intentions are good, outcomes can be misread. Leaders cannot control interpretation, but they can influence it by leading with steady behavior and clear communication. When reputation is strong, people approach the organization with belief rather than suspicion. When reputation is weak, every action is questioned."

Simon Whitehead's view of leadership is grounded in realism. "The world is fast. The world is loud. The world rewards leaders who can move quickly without losing themselves. Reputation is the force that makes this possible. It speeds belief. It gives people confidence that the leader's actions are rooted in principle. It turns complexity into something navigable."

This is why his perspective matters. Simon understands that modern leadership is not about control. It is about clarity. It is about steadiness. It is about the patterns leaders create through their choices. In a world that moves faster every year, reputation becomes the multiplier that helps leaders stay ahead of the moment rather than behind it.

More Than Message: The Research-Driven Reality of Reputation

INTERVIEW WITH TERRY NELSON, MANAGING PARTNER AT PLUS COMMUNICATIONS

Terry Nelson brings discipline and strategic clarity to some of the highest-pressure environments in public life: politics, corporate reputation, and crisis communications. At PLUS Communications, a bipartisan public affairs, strategic communications, and advertising firm, Terry has seen reputations rise and fall in real time and understands well how emotion, narrative, and behavior combine to shape perception. His political experience gives him an uncommon perspective on what moves people.

Terry's focus on preparation and message discipline offers lessons for any leader. "Reputation," he says, "is built through the habits that guide daily decisions, not through broad declarations or slogans. Credibility grows through consistent behavior and a clear sense of purpose."

Terry learned about reputation in a world where every decision plays out in public and every mistake has an audience—politics. It taught him that people respond not to what leaders intend, but to what leaders show. "It also taught me that narrative is not decoration. It is the structure through which people understand reality. Reputation has to live inside a narrative structure or it falls apart."

He speaks with the sharp clarity of someone who has spent years studying how people interpret information. "You have to start with what people actually believe," he says. "It's not what the organization wants them to believe. Not what leaders hope they believe. But what they believe already. That is where honesty begins." Terry does not sentimentalize this. He describes it as basic orientation. Leaders cannot influence perceptions they do not understand.

His world is built on discipline. He measures how messages land, how emotion shapes interpretation, and how context bends meaning. "I've led campaigns where timing mattered as much as language and where a single misread of the public mood could break momentum. Reputation is something gained slowly, lost quickly, and rebuilt through accuracy and responsibility."

Terry believes research is the ground beneath everything. "Research is the compass that keeps leaders from drifting into wishful thinking," he notes. "I've seen organizations convince themselves that their messages were working simply because they liked the messages. But the audience decides what matters. Leaders who ignore that reality create their own blind spots."

He explains that reputation is less about message than about meaning. "Messages are crafted. Meaning is earned," he believes. "People look for signals of competence, fairness, and steadiness. They pay attention to how leaders respond when events shift. They watch whether leaders accept responsibility or push it away. These signals shape reputation far more powerfully than any written statement."

In Terry's world, discipline is freedom. "When teams understand the purpose behind decisions, they act with sharper focus. When leaders communicate with clarity, confusion lifts. When the organization studies its audience, it stops speaking into the dark. This frees people to move with more confidence. Discipline is not restriction. It is direction," he has learned.

"Emotion plays a central role in shaping reputation," in Terry's opinion. "People rarely make judgments in neutral conditions. They respond to how leaders make them feel. Fear, pride, anxiety, hope, and frustration all influence how messages are heard. A leader's job is not to manipulate the emotion but to understand it. Emotion is information. Leaders who treat it as noise miss what matters most."

Terry has an unusual ability to simplify complexity without reducing it. He speaks about narrative the way engineers talk about structure. "Narrative holds everything in place. If the structure is weak, the story collapses. If the structure is strong, people feel steadier, even when the content is challenging." Terry believes leaders must learn to think this way because the world is too fast and too loud for them to improvise the story as they go.

"Reputation depends on how leaders show up in the difficult moments," says Terry. "Anyone can look confident when things are calm. People watch more closely when stakes rise. They notice how leaders treat their teams under pressure. They notice how leaders explain setbacks. They notice whether leaders hide behind language or use language to create understanding. These choices shape reputation more deeply than the moments leaders prepare for."

He also believes organizations underestimate how much repetition matters. "Not repetition as a marketing tactic, but repetition as reinforcement of principle," he emphasizes. "People learn what a leader stands for by seeing the same values expressed through different decisions. Leaders who change their message to suit the moment lose coherence. Leaders who stay rooted in principle create credibility."

Terry brings a sense of realism to everything he discusses. He does not imagine a world where leaders are perfect. "I work in a world where leaders are human and where mistakes are inevitable," he shares. "In my view, reputation becomes stronger when leaders acknowledge mistakes without defensiveness and correct them with clarity. People forgive error more readily than they forgive evasion."

Terry's political work taught him that every audience is fragmented. People bring different histories, hopes, and anxieties to the same story. A leader who wants to shape reputation must understand these differences. "One message rarely fits all. Good leaders adapt without losing their center. They speak to different audiences while expressing the same core identity," he advises.

Terry understands that research, message, and behavior form a triangle that supports or undermines reputation. When the three align, the organization moves with credibility. When they do not, the gaps become visible. He has spent his career closing those gaps so leaders can communicate with honesty and authority.

"Reputation is strengthened not by what leaders promise, but by what they prove," he believes. "Reputation is built through disciplined habits, clear thinking, and the willingness to see the world as it is, not as leaders wish it to be." Terry reminds us that reality is not the enemy. It is the foundation. When leaders embrace it, reputation becomes something earned, reliable, and real.

Beyond the Brand: What Politics Teaches Us About Reputation

INTERVIEW WITH JIM MARGOLIS, PARTNER AT GMMB

Jim Margolis has spent his career advising leaders in high-intensity situations—issue management, political strategy, and social impact campaigns. Jim understands how reputation is shaped in real time when every decision is visible and every audience has a point of view. His experience gives him a clear sense of how leaders earn credibility when the stakes are highest.

"Reputation is not a slogan," he says. "My work has shown me how reputational strength develops person by person and moment by moment."

Jim has sat beside leaders during the moments when everything is at risk. His perspective offers practical lessons for leaders who want to show up with confidence when it matters most. He has worked with candidates who became icons and candidates who fell apart under the weight of expectation. Through it all, he developed a clear view.

"People do not judge leaders on promises," he assures us. "They judge them on presence, tone, and the choices they make when pressure closes in. Reputation does not come from the brand a leader builds. It comes from how that leader behaves when people are watching or not."

He often describes politics as the most unforgiving test of leadership. "In politics, every word is recorded. Every moment is interpreted. Every hesitation becomes meaning," he says. "I learned that no amount of messaging can protect a leader who has not built the internal habits that earn credibility." He does not say it with judgment. He says it with the realism of experience. People respond to leaders who are steady, authentic, and emotionally grounded.

Jim has spent decades helping leaders understand how audiences form impressions. "Reputation is a long arc, shaped by patterns rather than moments," he shares. "A speech can move people for a day. Behavior moves people for a lifetime."

Leaders who think of reputation as a campaign create distance between themselves and the people they hope to influence. Leaders who think of reputation as character create connection.

He tells stories of sitting with candidates who were exhausted from the pace of the trail. "We spend days filled with town halls, debates, interviews, and relentless scrutiny. Some become defensive. Some become rehearsed. The ones who hold steady are the ones who understand that leadership is a human act. They speak with a sense of purpose that doesn't wobble when the moments get hard."

The public wants leaders who tell the truth about what they know and what they do not yet know. "People want confidence without arrogance and optimism without fantasy," he says. He has seen leaders lose credibility because they tried to project certainty when uncertainty was the honest answer. "People can handle the truth," he says. "What they cannot handle is feeling manipulated." Honesty becomes a reputational advantage because it gives people something solid to hold.

Politics sharpen a leader's awareness of audience. "No leader speaks to a single public. People carry different fears, hopes, and experiences into the same moment," he says. "I learned to read these emotional currents and help leaders speak in ways that reach across difference without erasing complexity."

He believes organizations can learn from this. Reputation depends on recognizing that people are not abstract stakeholders. They are individuals with perspectives shaped by their own lives.

Jim does not romanticize political communication. He sees the machinery behind it. The research, the targeting, the testing. But he also sees that none of it matters if the leader is not grounded. Voters feel when the person is uncertain or disconnected, or whether they're confident, calm, and real. That emotional truth is what strengthens or weakens reputation.

One of Jim's strongest beliefs is that leaders cannot separate message from behavior. "Message can clarify behavior. It cannot replace it. Leaders who try to control the narrative without controlling their actions create a credibility gap that grows with every inconsistency. The public might forgive mistakes, but they rarely forgive patterns of behavior that feel careless or self-serving. Reputation grows when leaders behave in ways that give meaning to their own words," he firmly states.

He learned that momentum in politics often comes from small human moments that reveal character. "It's a conversation with a voter. A moment of humility during a debate. A quiet act of fairness that shifts how people perceive the leader. These moments cannot be scripted. They come from the leader's internal compass," he says. "Organizations should pay attention to these cues. They tell the real story of who the leader is."

Jim also recognizes that political storytelling requires discipline. "Leaders must explain where they are going and why it matters. They must do it clearly, consistently, and without talking down to people. Businesses can use the same discipline to build reputations that endure. People want to understand the logic behind decisions. They want to see the values that guide those decisions. When leaders explain these things with care, they create stability even in volatile environments."

He has watched leaders navigate crises that could have destroyed their reputations. "The ones who survived did not hide. They showed up with honesty and responsibility. They faced the moment instead of avoiding it. They acknowledged mistakes and explained how they would correct them," he says. "This willingness to be accountable is one of the most powerful forces in reputation building."

In his view, reputation becomes the throughline of a leader's story. "Reputation connects past behavior to present decisions and future promises. It creates continuity. It helps people interpret events without jumping to fear or suspicion. When reputation is strong, people approach the leader with a sense of belief rather than doubt. That belief speeds everything around the leader. Decisions move faster. Communication lands more clearly. Teams feel steadier."

Jim Margolis brings the realism of politics to any conversation about leadership. He understands that leaders cannot expect people to accept their narratives without earning them. He knows that reputation grows from the inside out, through the steady choices leaders make in full view of the people they serve. His experience in politics offers a lesson that applies everywhere. The brand is not the story. Behavior is. And when behavior is grounded and consistent, reputation becomes something real, reliable, and lasting.

Reputation as a System, Not a Campaign

INTERVIEW WITH ROBIN CALLIF, GLOBAL CHIEF STRATEGY OFFICER AT OMNICOM PUBLIC RELATIONS

"If there's one thing I've learned after decades working with C-suites," says Robin Callif, "it's this: Most leaders want to believe that reputation is something they can manage with the right message. That a strong campaign, a rebrand, or a great piece of content will set the record straight. But here's the truth—and it's a hard one: You can't campaign your way out of a systems problem."

That's why I turned to Robin for this chapter. She's not here to make you feel better. She's here to make you see better, based on her observations over a career in public relations, advertising, and public affairs.

Robin looks at reputation like an architect looks at a skyscraper: not at the glossy exterior but at the structural integrity underneath. She knows that what ultimately shapes a brand's reputation isn't the tagline or the logo—it's the governance, culture, decisions, and daily behaviors that sit behind it: the system.

"Too many leaders treat reputation as a communications problem," says Robin. "But it's a leadership system problem. One that's fixable—but only if you're willing to stop thinking episodically and start thinking systemically."

In our conversation, she makes a compelling case for why coherence is the new competitive advantage and why organizations that fail to integrate their actions with their ambitions will eventually pay the price. Not just in headlines—but in lost trust, market drag, and cultural confusion.

Robin sees the load-bearing beams, the joints, the seams, and the places where stress accumulates. She sees how decisions made in one corner of a company echo across the entire structure. Most leaders, she says, think of reputation as something they can shape with messages. Robin has spent her career helping them understand the systems that support reputation.

"Reputation is not a campaign," she says with calm certainty. "It is not a one-off action. It is the output of governance, culture, product, and leadership."

The line is crisp because it comes from long experience. She has watched companies try to solve systemic issues with quick messaging fixes. She has watched leaders mistake visibility for impact. And she has watched the same leaders realize, sometimes painfully, that the public does not separate the press release from the behavior behind it.

"Reputation strengthens when leaders think holistically across their entire organizational chart," she explains. "Most organizations respond to reputational pressure with moments of focus: a report here, a crisis response there, a marketing sprint to regain favor. These moments matter, but they do not add up unless they sit inside a larger system of values, decisions, and habits. Reputation is a continuous feedback loop, not a static thing."

Her clarity comes from years helping clients understand what drives stakeholder judgment. She sees reputation as a multiplier that accelerates business performance when everything is aligned. "A strong reputation compounds growth by lifting confidence across customers, employees, investors, and regulators. A weak reputation becomes a drag on performance, a kind of invisible tax that slows progress," she says. "Reputation is like a hidden profit and loss statement—on one side, a good reputation compounds across the business; on the other, a bad one is a drag on results."

Robin often explains that leaders tend to underestimate the integration required to build a coherent story. "Companies hire agencies for brand, for reputation, for public affairs, as if each lives in its own universe. In truth, the lines between these fields have collapsed. Reputation influences brand. Brand influences public affairs. Public affairs influences a company's license to operate, which shapes everything else," she reveals.

"For years, clients had to stitch this integration together on their own," she says. "But that burden is unreasonable. Organizations like Omnicom Public Relations create value by connecting these disciplines through shared insight, measurement, and system design. Nothing needs to live in isolation anymore."

What she is describing is not efficiency. It is coherence. "Reputation breaks when different parts of the company express different interpretations of who and what the company is. Customers sense the fracture. Regulators sense it. Employees sense it most of all.

Integration is not about uniformity. It is about alignment between behavior and ambition."

Robin explains that many leaders still treat trust as the goal. "Trust is one of the inputs, but reputation is the output. Trust lives in individual relationships. A consumer trusts a product. An employee trusts a manager. An investor trusts a forecast. Reputation is the collective view of the whole enterprise. Trust alone does not deliver an outcome," she says. "Reputation is the system where it all comes together."

This systemic view changes how leaders think about strategy. It shifts the focus from marketing to management, from optics to operations. "A company cannot claim innovation if its governance does not reward the behaviors that produce innovation," she emphasizes. "Communications can only amplify what the company proves through its actions. If it's not systematized, then it's BS. To be innovative, you have to do innovative things."

Her candor is not harsh; it is clarifying. Robin believes leaders deserve honesty about what truly drives reputation. "My role is helping clients understand the patterns, incentives, and cultural choices that shape how the world interprets them. Reputation is built whether leaders think about it or not. The question is whether it is built intentionally or by accident."

Robin's view of the future is unambiguous. "Reputation work will become more integrated, more data driven, and more systemic. AI will knit together insights that once lived in separate corners of the organization. Networks of specialists will operate from shared dashboards and common frameworks. Leaders will have clearer visibility into how behavior compounds into perception," she maintains.

"Reputation becomes real when it reflects the true structure of the organization. When leaders align their ambition with their actions, reputation becomes a source of propulsion. It pulls the company forward. It strengthens the license to operate. It gives meaning to the story the organization tells about itself," she believes.

Robin sees reputation clearly because she sees systems clearly. She shows leaders how to build reputations that endure, not through campaigns, but through coherence, alignment, and the steady work of making sure the organization behaves the way it wants to be seen.

For Robin, this brings discipline to a field that has long depended on instinct. It creates accountability. It connects culture, governance, communication, and performance through measurable outcomes. Most of all, it reminds leaders that reputation is not something they own. It is something they earn, through the systems they create and the choices they make every day.

Part III

THE TACTICAL PLAYBOOK

Chapter 13

THE NEW REPUTATION JOURNEY

What does today's reputation journey look like?

The crisp, clean stages of awareness, consideration, and decision-making no longer reflect how people move through the world. Instead, we're navigating a messy, nonlinear landscape shaped by fragmentation, cultural shifts, and real-time emotional reactions. So how do we build (or rebuild) reputation in this kind of terrain?

Today, reputation rarely follows a clean progression. Instead, it loops. A TikTok clip, a friend's recommendation, a review on Amazon, or a critical article might all collide in the same hour. What was once sequential is now simultaneous, fragmented, and recursive.

This shift doesn't just affect marketing departments; it rewrites the assumptions leaders make about how trust is built and maintained. A single weak signal can shift the entire loop, while a well-timed, credible act can reinforce it for months or years.

Leaders who continue to plan around neat stages risk building campaigns that look elegant on paper but collapse in practice when confronted with the reality of today's culture-driven dynamics.

Three Questions That Anchor the Journey

If the old, linear funnel no longer applies, what replaces it? At its core, the reputation journey now begins with three deceptively simple questions:

- Who are you?
- What are you known for?
- What do you stand for?

They are not checklist items; they are the baseline for credibility—the foundation of the entire reputation journey. Without clear answers to these questions, reputation becomes brittle. With clarity, however, reputational momentum builds quickly and sustainably.

These questions are not only philosophical; they are operational. They drive decisions about product design, customer engagement, and even employee behavior. We return to these themes in Chapter 15, where we explore expectation and experience in more detail. There, you'll see how the principles behind the three questions translate from strategic foundation into lived reputation outcomes.

Culture as a Gravitational Force

In today's environment, culture is the true gravitational force that binds reputations together. Demographics are blunt instruments—age, income, or geography cannot fully explain why people trust, engage, or advocate. Culture can.

Culture shows up in the memes people share, the fandoms they join, the values they project, and the communities they build. These signals cut across traditional boundaries, aligning strangers through shared meaning. If your strategy ignores cultural context, it will miss the gravitational pull that holds reputations in orbit.

The gravitational metaphor is no accident. Culture exerts a steady force, pulling audiences toward or away from your brand. Leaders who fail to read cultural signals will find themselves drifting into irrelevance, no matter how robust their marketing expenditure. Culture creates cohesion in fragmented environments, giving reputations a center of gravity.

When Journeys Become Ripples

Reputations are increasingly shaped by cultural ripples that extend far beyond original intentions.

- A film like *KPop Demon Hunters* sparks a global fandom that drives music charts as much as movie tickets.
- A video game like *Kingdom Come: Deliverance* transforms regional tourism economies.

- Nike's bet on Michael Jordan didn't just save a business line—it reset the template for athlete-brand partnerships.

These examples prove that reputation journeys are not confined to campaigns. They spill over into culture, commerce, and even civic life. A creative choice that begins as a brand expression can evolve into a movement, influencing behavior, reshaping industries, and creating long-term loyalty.

The lesson is clear: Reputations don't live in silos. They move outward in waves, influenced by countless cultural interactions. Leaders who understand this ripple effect can seed actions that travel further than any paid campaign ever could.

Navigating the New Journey

If culture and signals define the new reputation journey, leaders need new tools to navigate it. One structural solution is the cross-functional Reputation Council—a standing team that scans cultural shifts, decodes weak signals, and aligns responses across marketing, PR, legal, HR, and the C-suite.

The council does more than manage crises. It democratizes reputation. It creates shared ownership and ensures agility. By connecting insights across departments, it prevents leaders from flying blind in turbulent environments.

The Reputation Council can also serve as an early-warning radar if team members can spot cultural changes on the horizon and prepare coordinated responses before reputational risks escalate. Just as a national security council connects intelligence from across agencies, a Reputation Council unifies organizational awareness, ensuring leaders act on culture with speed and coherence.

Believability as the Final Test

In the end, reputation journeys live or die on believability. Audiences are overwhelmed by information and competing truths. They no longer assume alignment between messaging and behavior; they demand proof. A narrative that does not match lived experience will collapse.

Believability is not about perfection; it's about consistency. Audiences will forgive mistakes if they see accountability and alignment. They will not forgive hypocrisy. When what you say and what you do diverge, trust evaporates.

That is why today's reputation journey is not simply about what you say but whether audiences believe what they see and feel. Culture provides the context. Leadership provides the judgment. Together, they create reputational patterns that endure, shaping not just attention but long-term trust.

TAKEAWAYS

- *Retire* the linear funnel—today's reputation journey is circular, fragmented, and recursive.
- *Anchor* every strategy in three core questions: Who are you? What are you known for? What do you stand for?

- *Decode* cultural signals—memes, fandoms, and shared values drive alignment more than demographics.
- *Leverage* cultural ripples; bold creative acts often produce reputational momentum far beyond original plans.
- *Build* structural agility—cross-functional Reputation Councils connect signals to strategy in real time.
- *Test* every narrative for believability; alignment between words and actions is the final measure of credibility.

Chapter 14

THE CRAFT AND DISCIPLINE OF REPUTATIONAL IMPACT

Great PR and great reputations are built on the fusion of creativity and credibility. Creativity generates the moments that audiences remember; credibility gives those moments staying power. Without creativity, PR risks becoming formulaic and forgettable. Without credibility, creativity becomes empty theater. The real magic happens when both forces work together, amplifying each other in ways that not only earn attention but also sustain trust and reputation over time.

A standout example is Old Spice, a heritage brand that rebooted its identity with surreal humor and bold absurdity. Recognizing that 60 percent of body wash purchases were made by women, the brand promised "the man your man could smell like," creating a conversation among couples rather than a traditional "men's product" pitch and featuring horses, boats, diamonds, and parodied masculinity. They didn't tone down the weird.

They dialed in to reset expectations, build buzz, and command attention. Crazy? Yes! The result was a viral reset: Within just a week, the "Man Your Man Could Smell Like" ad amassed over 40 million YouTube views and had eight of the eleven most-viewed videos online. Body wash sales surged by more than 60 percent in just three months and then more than 125 percent year over year, propelling Old Spice to the top of the US men's body wash market. Meanwhile, their digital footprint exploded: Twitter followers rose 2,700 percent, Facebook engagement climbed 800 percent, and website traffic tripled.[1] That's a long-game payoff: They leaned into offbeat creativity, leaned into real-time digital engagement, and stuck with it.

Practicing the Craft, Leading with Discipline

PR and reputation strategy are practices, not perfect sciences. Like medicine, they blend art, judgment, data, and experience. You don't always know what will work, but you commit to learning, adjusting, and moving forward. You build best practices and you also take risks. You measure outcomes, you see what works and what doesn't. You stay alert, adapt in real time, and never lose sight of the bigger story you're telling. It takes courage, especially in a world measured in clicks, likes, and quarterly results.

That's why PR should be practiced like a craft and led like a discipline. It's iterative, adaptive, and rooted in both art and analysis. The best PR leaders combine the instincts of a storyteller with the precision of a strategist: They can read a cultural moment, anticipate how it will evolve, and design a narrative that travels well across audiences and channels. They understand that the story is not just what you tell but how you act—and that the most reputationally valuable actions are often the most creatively daring.

That requires a commitment to listening as much as speaking. The listening informs the creativity; the creativity drives the connection; the connection strengthens the reputation.

Creativity Is a Human Strength: Use It to Your Advantage

The future of reputation will belong to practitioners who can operate in this blended space—who can move fluidly between data dashboards and creative brainstorms, between high-level strategy sessions and on-the-ground cultural insight. These are the leaders who will see patterns before others do, take calculated creative risks, and turn those risks into reputational advantages.

In the end, reputation strategy is more than a business discipline—it's a human one. We tend to frame creativity as the property of "creatives" or the marketing department, but as the famed record producer Rick Rubin reminds us, everyone is a creator.[2] Creativity isn't a rare gift or a job title; it's a way of paying attention, of choosing deliberately, of shaping the conditions for trust and connection. Every choice we make, attuned or careless, is a form of self-expression. In the context of reputation, those choices accumulate into the narratives we create. They also shape and influence the opinions that audiences develop based on their own experiences with the brand.

That's why the most effective reputation leaders see themselves not only as strategists but also as curators of experience. They understand that in every micro-moment (whether in a boardroom, on a factory floor, or in the comment section), they are shaping the world their audiences perceive. They practice creativity by refining their sensitivity to what resonates and what repels.

Ultimately, creativity is the force that turns reputation from a defensive shield into a source of momentum. It's how leaders transform scattered impressions into coherent narratives and fleeting interactions into durable relationships. The future won't reward the loudest voices or the biggest budgets; it will reward those who can combine cultural awareness with creative discipline and who use that blend to earn attention, loyalty, and influence. In reputation work, creativity isn't the garnish on the plate. It is the main ingredient, the advantage that sets enduring leaders and enduring brands apart.

TAKEAWAYS

- *Blend* creativity with discipline; great PR is craft, not magic.
- *Track* signals constantly; let audience behavior guide story adjustments.
- *Align* campaigns with actions; credibility collapses if stories outpace reality.

- *Recognize* that PR leaders are both strategists and storytellers.
- *Ensure* each campaign builds lasting credibility, not just momentary buzz.

Chapter 15

REPUTATION LIVES WHERE EXPECTATION AND EXPERIENCE MEET

Reputation is how people perceive you. It's what others experience, share, and internalize about you or your brand. Reputation is shaped less by planned campaigns and more by the complex pathways people take as they navigate digital space every day. And as someone who interacts with brands both virtually and in the real world, I've come to believe that a brand's reputation begins forming long before a company even realizes it.

Take Uber, for example. I didn't hear about it through an ad. I heard about it from a colleague at a party. It was pure word of mouth. I remember thinking, *What's an Uber?* But the concept caught my interest, and I explored it myself. That journey from curiosity to loyal user was driven entirely by experience. Uber promised clean, timely rides. And when they slipped, they fixed it. They delivered. For me, that's what sealed their reputation and earned my loyalty.

Same with Amazon. Like most people, I've never been to an Amazon store. But Amazon is one of the most present brands in my life. The convenience, the clarity, the customer service—it all adds up. Amazon's reputation isn't built on ads. It's built on every seamless transaction. That's how I know who they are. That's why I trust them.

Then there's Peloton. I joined because people told me I'd love it. I stayed because the brand created an experience I could rely on. Even when I drifted back to outdoor biking after the pandemic, I felt like I was betraying a friend. That's the level of emotional connection Peloton created—one that didn't rely on a storefront or a handshake, just consistency and community.

I've had negative experiences with brands, too. A famous New York City restaurant with five-star reviews but also with a rude waiter won't see me again. There are subscription services that don't deliver and are completely unreachable when customers need to communicate with them. No brand is perfect, but each interaction decides whether you'll have more or less revenue by the end of the quarter.

The modern reputation journey isn't a carefully planned route from Point A to Point Z. It can be a meandering path through social media, celebrity influencers, and everyday conversations. It locks in when experience aligns with expectation. That first encounter may come from an offhand comment by a friend mentioning a new product in a group chat. But that's just the beginning. Once you actually try the product or service, its reputation gels and solidifies. Was the experience good? Did the brand deliver on its promise? If yes, a good reputation emerges. If the experience falls short, the brand's reputation is tarnished, and it will take more than just talk to repair it; people will actually avoid the brand.

That said, the perceived connection between a brand and its reputation can be convoluted. If you love Harry Potter, does that mean you endorse every controversial tweet J. K. Rowling posts? And if you vibe with Beyoncé's music but roll your eyes when she gets letters from PETA, does that diminish your admiration for her as a performer or make you less of a fan? Our relationships with brands are often complicated and cannot be reduced to simple formulas.

We used to think we could control reputation with messaging. We can't. We can shape it through expectations and experience. That's why platforms like Instagram and YouTube matter—not because they sell products, but because they set expectations. The content people see there frames the mindset they bring into the first brand interaction.

And this isn't just about business-to-consumer (B2C) transactions. There's a growing conversation about how this applies to business-to-business (B2B) and business-to-government (B2G). The stakes are higher, the risks are greater, but the fundamentals are the same. Reputation is earned through trust, reliability, and delivering on promises, whether you're selling bikes or cloud solutions. Today, the journey is mostly virtual, shaped by mobile devices and filtered through social platforms. That's where opinions are formed, shared, and amplified. If we want to lead in reputation strategy, we have to show up authentically in that space. We have to deliver consistently, digitally and personally.

Reputation is no longer a slogan or a tagline; it's the expectation of an experience. And that experience had better be aligned with the promise, or your audiences will head for the hills.

TAKEAWAYS

- *Audit* the expectations being set for your brand across social platforms, influencers, and cultural conversations.
- *Align* delivery with those expectations at every touchpoint—loyalty is earned when promises match reality.
- *Measure* customer experience continuously; each interaction either deposits or withdraws from your reputation account.
- *Recognize* that word of mouth often outperforms advertising; invest in experiences that people want to share.
- *Apply* the same discipline across B2C, B2B, and B2G markets—expectations and delivery drive reputation everywhere.

Chapter 16

REPUTATION INTELLIGENCE IS RISK MANAGEMENT IN REAL TIME

Because of my long experience in corporate public relations and crisis management, I naturally tend to view reputation from a corporate business perspective. Moreover, I am an early pioneer in the field of reputation intelligence, which I define as a data-driven system for making critical decisions about managing reputation. It's a scientific process of gathering, analyzing, and interpreting data about an individual's or organization's reputation in the public sphere. The goal of reputation intelligence is understanding the current state of a firm's reputation *and* predicting potential changes or threats based on emerging trends and public sentiment.

Reputation intelligence is a proactive approach that monitors reputation in real time; it helps businesses or individuals anticipate risks, adapt to changing conditions, and avoid catastrophic losses.

I'm a strong proponent of reputation intelligence because I know from experience that it can elevate business value by improving customer sentiment, preventing crises, enhancing brand equity, increasing operational efficiency, and maintaining investor confidence. The proactive use of reputation intelligence enables companies to preserve market value, mitigate crises, and enhance brand loyalty. The ability to turn data into actionable strategies to protect or build a company's reputation is increasingly seen as a competitive advantage in today's lightning-quick and globally interconnected digital markets and economies.

Reputation intelligence is an ensemble of data-driven processes. Measurement techniques include social media reach, share of voice, sentiment analysis, media analysis, and stakeholder surveys. You can also gauge a company's reputation by looking at "proxy" metrics such as its stock price and current market capitalization, revenue growth and profitability over time, credit ratings (issued by agencies like Moody's and S&P), customer satisfaction scores, and employee satisfaction and retention rates. If you're looking for a general indication of a company's workplace culture, you can check Glassdoor and Indeed. There are also comprehensive proprietary models such as RepTrak, Reputation Score, Net Promoter Score (NPS), and Reputation Quotient (RQ).

Suffice it to say that processes and techniques for measuring and analyzing reputation are continually adapting and evolving to keep pace with the dizzying speed of change in our media and communication landscapes.

Earlier in this book, I mention that it's become impossible to keep secrets in our hyperconnected, AI-empowered society. But that doesn't mean you have to go around blurting everything you know. Managing reputation successfully requires a degree of discipline and self-censorship. Sometimes, silence is golden. And most of the time, less is more.

I have a good friend who was the media relations manager at a large healthcare insurance company. He was on the front lines when, for a variety of complicated reasons, the company's stock price cratered, plummeting within the span of a few weeks from over $90 to under $10 a share. For years, the company had been a darling of Wall Street. Then suddenly it became a pariah. As you can imagine, the media coverage was merciless. Here's how my friend remembers those harrowing days:

> We had a great reputation and a resilient business model, but the erasure of that much corporate wealth in such a short period of time was shocking. I had a list of four bullet points that had been written by a team of seasoned PR consultants and vetted by a team of expert Wall Street lawyers. For the next six months after our stock crashed, I stuck to those four bullet points, repeating them endlessly to every journalist who called or emailed me. The only time I departed from the script, our stock price dropped again, but only briefly. I stuck to the four bullet points faithfully after that. Over time, we righted the ship, and eventually we were acquired by a larger company, thanks in no small part to our reputation in the healthcare insurance market and our tightly disciplined response to the crisis.

TAKEAWAYS

- *Invest* in reputation intelligence systems that track sentiment in real time.
- *Integrate* data from media, stakeholders, and platforms to anticipate threats.
- *Align* decision-making with reputational signals, not just financial forecasts.
- *Predict* shifts in perception early, and adjust strategy before crises emerge.
- *Treat* reputation intelligence as a discipline—rely on evidence, not intuition.

Chapter 17

MICRO-MOMENTS, MACRO IMPACT: REPUTATION AT THE SPEED OF CULTURE

It's indisputable that the practice of building and managing reputation has evolved more rapidly than anyone expected. Leaders who fail to adapt will be sidelined as others define the narrative.

Staying in the game means embracing a new set of operational standards based less on static principles and more on rapid improvisation. Media is now fragmented, omnichannel *and* omnipresent. As a result, the power of brands to control messaging has been reduced drastically.

The new reality compels us to rethink how we define audiences and how we communicate with them. And it leads to genuinely difficult questions, such as "How do we operationalize reputation strategies for audiences that no longer fit comfortably into traditional buckets of age, race, education, gender, geography, economic status, and other conventional measures?"

People swipe, scroll, engage, forget, and reengage. They constantly switch roles, shifting effortlessly from consumer to critic to creator. In fact, user-created content can be more influential than a brand's formal marketing campaigns. Social media algorithms accelerate and expand the spread of content, whether it's "officially" scripted or created on the spur of the moment by someone with a clever idea.

This environment isn't a funnel; it's a swirl of influence, fueled by unpredictable, emotionally charged micro-moments. And these moments don't just disrupt old models of marketing—they redefine the terrain of reputation itself. In this new era, reputation isn't something you shape with messaging alone; it's something you earn or lose in all of the spaces where people are paying attention. That's why today's reputation strategy is about recognizing signals, responding to them, and keeping the right message visible when it matters most.

The rise of micro-influencers, private chat groups, and anonymous moderators means that the people shaping your reputation may not be part of your customer relationship management (CRM). A CFO might also be a meme lord. A retiree might be a crypto enthusiast. People don't live in buckets; nor are they one-dimensional. They live in fluid, overlapping realities. Nevertheless, these people influencing your reputation have always been out there, and now they're playing increasingly active roles in how consumers decide to interact with brands like yours.

I don't see this as a moment of crisis; I see it as a moment of clarity. Reputation is more than a simple linear construct that unfolds gradually over time; it's a complex, dynamic system of relationships, signals, and stories in motion. If we're serious about protecting and growing reputational value, we need to start listening better, thinking more broadly, and moving faster. We can't be just talking *at* people. We should be talking *with* people, engaging with their views and building trust.

Smart reputation practitioners are investing in AI tools that help them track real-time sentiment, identify emotionally charged micro-moments, and determine which way their audience is trending. They're not waiting for opinion polls or Q4 focus groups. They're watching public group chats, analyzing reaction emojis, and mapping narratives as they evolve and sprint across multiple platforms.

If you're looking for your audience where they *used to be*, you're already too late. Reputation strategy is all about following the motion, listening to the signals, and being ready to meet consumers where they are now—even if it's not where you expected.

Think of a viral customer complaint, a CEO's offhand comment during a livestream, or a reaction video that unexpectedly blows up. Or the kid who accidentally becomes the face of a meme. These aren't planned campaigns; they're unforeseen and unpredictable blips that shoot past the traditional filters and reshape perceptions with dizzying speed. Sometimes these micro-moments are silly and amusing, and sometimes they are shocking and disturbing. In some cases, they even disrupt our assumptions and create new memories with lingering power. The thing that hasn't changed is that negative emotions are stronger and more memorable than the positive ones, and a single disappointing experience can have a bigger impact than a hundred positive ones.

Behavioral data is more accessible than ever, but you have to use it. If you can see how opinions are forming and sentiment is shifting in real time, you can start to map your reputational risks and opportunities with far more precision.

Your reputation is not window dressing. It's leverage. Credibility is currency. And no, this isn't just an organic unraveling of the social contract. It's curated and incentivized. Loyalty converts, and engagement pays. Algorithms are not neutral. Reputation isn't a bug; it's a feature that's baked into the model.

It's All About Responsiveness

There was a time when managing reputation meant crafting a perfect message, locking it down, and sending it out to a credulous world. Today, brand narratives are discovered through audience interactions rather than through direct brand messaging. And audiences aren't shy about re-creating and repurposing brand messaging. The traditional formats of engagement have become increasingly interactive and more challenging to control. Opinions are formed through real-time interactions and audience responses that can be difficult to predict.

Mindlessly copying something that has worked for the company in the past or for another brand is a recipe for failure. That's why modern reputation strategy needs to move away from rigid messaging frameworks and toward something more fluid and adaptive. *Orchestration* is the term some experts use, but it sounds a little too formal for the messy reality of modern communication. What we're talking about is a shift from broadcasting to listening, from control to coordination.

Audiences expect brands to appear consistently across platforms, yet not in a robotic manner. That means coordination across teams (communications, HR, marketing, legal) so responses feel unified, even when they're coming from different voices on different platforms.

Reputational wins don't come solely from saying the "right thing" at the "right time." They come from teams who are tuned in, sharing what they're hearing and making fast decisions together. Context is king, and a message that felt perfect yesterday might feel tone-deaf today, even if it has been meticulously planned and preapproved by the brand.

Continuous Real-Time Storytelling

Your brand story isn't a movie with a script. It's a live show with an audience of real human beings who make decisions and reach conclusions. You don't get to control how people receive your message, only how well you adapt in the moment. The best reputation strategists keep their hand on the volume dial and the tone knob, adjusting and fine-tuning when needed.

Successful brands can detect subtle shifts in sentiment and opinion and artfully modulate their responses in sympathy with the reactions they're detecting. This is much more than simple messaging; it's signal matching.

If the old model was conducting a symphony where everyone followed a sheet of music in perfect unison, the new model is more like a jam session. People take turns, they improvise, and they listen to what's happening in the social channels they are spending most of their time in.

Today's audiences already know what they want, and if you don't deliver on their expectations, you're replaced in a matter of seconds. This is particularly relevant for brands targeting younger generations, whose spending power is rapidly increasing.

Reputation isn't about memorizing the right lines; it's about knowing how to respond when the lights suddenly change or the audience asks a hard question. Brands that stick too closely to a script risk sounding out of touch. The ones that win are those that sound human, complete with foibles and occasional mistakes. The brands that protect and grow their reputation will be the ones who know how to listen, pivot, and respond in real time, with a combination of integrity and improvisational flair.

TAKEAWAYS

- *Listen* to your audiences in real time; track sentiment shifts daily through social feeds, group chats, and micro-signals.
- *Map* influence beyond demographics; follow behaviors across fluid, overlapping communities.
- *Train* your team to respond in hours, not weeks; delay equals irrelevance.
- *Equip* reputation managers with AI tools that surface emotional micro-moments before they escalate.
- *Treat* every audience interaction as a test of credibility; people decide in seconds whether to engage, ignore, or walk away.

Chapter 18

REPUTATION REWARDS THE BRAVE: WHY CREATIVITY IS A BUSINESS IMPERATIVE

We talk a lot about creativity in our industry. We use it to capture attention, spark emotions, connect with audiences, and drive cultural relevance. But creativity doesn't stand alone. Without the weight of a strong reputation, even the most brilliant ideas can fall flat. The real power comes from pairing creativity with a credible reputation strategy to deliver results that last. Creativity, reputation, and impact aren't separate pillars—they're parts of a single, living ecosystem.

Each fuels the other in an endless loop: Creativity builds reputation, reputation drives results, and results fuel the confidence to create the next big thing. In today's communications landscape, these forces are codependent and inseparable. Brands that fail to integrate them risk becoming irrelevant in a culture that demands authenticity, relevance, and meaning in every micro-moment.

Viewed from this perspective, creativity isn't a bonus or an add-on; it's the main artery through which reputation and results flow. Outsourcing creativity might seem like a convenience, but the risks outweigh the momentary rewards.

As Jean-Marie Dru argues in *Beyond Disruption*, the most transformative ideas don't just improve the status quo; they redefine it.[1] He points to Dick Fosbury, who revolutionized high jumping with his unusual "Fosbury Flop"—going over the bar backward instead of forward.[2] What began as a creative workaround became the dominant technique in his sport. In the same way, brands that dare to challenge conventions can set new standards for entire industries.

Meanwhile, the renewed cultural appetite for sincerity (it's cool to care again) underscores how audiences increasingly favor authenticity over irony, and values over cleverness.[3] PR and storytelling must reflect that shift by aligning creativity with genuine human concern, not just brand positioning.

Even as AI reshapes our workflows, it cannot replace the strategic judgment that turns noise into meaning. As one communication veteran observes, "AI can help you get to the right result, but it can't tell you what the right result is."[4] That distinction is critical. Creativity must be grounded in purpose.

Together, these perspectives reinforce a key premise: Creativity is not an ornament for PR—it's the catalyst for credibility, resonance, and long-term relevance. When ideas are fresh and original, people believe the brand behind them has vision and conviction. Creativity signals that you're not recycling old playbooks but leading with intent, which gives your message weight. In a noisy environment, it's creativity that makes your story feel credible and worth remembering. In an era defined by skepticism and rapid digital spread, reputation wins go to those who dare to be deeply curious, genuinely caring, and strategically intentional.

Too often, we silo creativity inside the marketing department or outsource it to an ad agency. But creativity is a strategic resource. It's not icing on the cake; it's the cake itself. Creativity isn't always about dazzling visuals or clever slogans. It can mean great timing, the right choice of words, or an unplanned human gesture that sparks connection and inspires action. Meaningful results often come from aligning creativity, authenticity, and purpose, even when it means stepping off the safe, familiar path.

Reputation challenges emerge in real time, across unpredictable contexts. A viral tweet, an offhand remark that ignites backlash, a YouTube parody—these moments call for interpretation, not templated responses. That's where creativity earns its seat at the table. Not as decoration, but as problem-solving that elevates credibility and accelerates brand relevance.

But to get there, leaders must undergo a mindset shift, one that redefines their role from message managers to *narrative architects and creative strategists*.

TAKEAWAYS

- *Link* creativity with credibility; one without the other fails.

- *Encourage* bold ideas that align with brand values and reputation equity.

- *Measure* creative success not just in awards but in reputational outcomes.
- *Invest* in ideas that generate both cultural impact and market growth.
- *Treat* creativity as a driver of resilience, not just differentiation.

Chapter 19

OMNICHANNEL COMMUNICATIONS: ONE REPUTATION, EVERYWHERE, ALL AT ONCE

Reputation today is shaped by a world that refuses to stay in its lanes. Channels blend. Boundaries blur. A message that begins on TikTok is echoed on LinkedIn, questioned in a private Slack group, repeated by analysts, and interpreted again by a language model before leadership has time to scan the morning headlines. The velocity is unmistakable. Yet the deeper challenge is not speed but the growing inability to predict how information will travel and how meaning will shift as it moves.

For leaders, this environment demands a more holistic mindset. Reputation can no longer be protected by a single team or expressed through a single path. It is touched by every conversation, every stakeholder, every system, and every surface where the organization shows up. An omnichannel strategy is not a luxury. It is a requirement for operating with coherence in a world where the narrative evolves in real time.

What has become clear to me in working with leadership teams is that omnichannel strategy does not begin with channels. It begins with clarity. Before organizations map platforms or plan content, they must define the center that will hold everything together. This is the foundation. It is the meaning that does not move, the behavior that does not waver, and the proof that does not erode under pressure. In a fragmented world, the foundation becomes the strongest form of unity an organization can have.

An effective omnichannel strategy builds outward from this center. It creates consistency across functions. It shapes how teams behave. It provides discipline around decisions. Most of all, it ensures that no matter where a stakeholder encounters the brand, the experience feels authentic and aligned. Reputational strength emerges not from the volume of communication but from the coherence of it.

The following pages explore this system and show how leaders can bring it to life.

The Foundation: Defining the Organization

A strong omnichannel reputation system begins with the foundation. This is the single most important element and, in practice, the one most often overlooked. The foundation is the shared identity, meaning, and behavioral evidence that define what the organization represents. It must remain visible and consistent across every channel. When fully built, it becomes the organization's operating center of gravity.

The foundation contains five essential elements: (1) enduring meaning, (2) alignment between values and behavior, (3) AI-aware, (4) internal alignment, and (5) the present and future storyline.

ENDURING MEANING

Every organization that thrives over time possesses a small set of truths that do not change. These truths create familiarity. They build emotional connection. They make the organization legible in a world overloaded with signals. Leaders must define what these truths are. Without them, omnichannel activity becomes a collection of disconnected outputs rather than a unified expression of purpose.

Enduring meaning is not marketing language. It is not a tagline. It is the deeper promise that the organization keeps with its stakeholders. It explains what the brand stands for in a way that feels real and recognizable. When people encounter the brand in any channel, they should be able to say, without effort, that they know exactly what it represents.

These enduring elements may evolve, but they do not disappear. They form a throughline across generations of products, leadership teams, and market cycles. When these elements are unclear, fragmentation follows. When they are strong, they become a strategic asset in every environment.

ALIGNMENT BETWEEN VALUES AND BEHAVIOR

A foundation built only on statements has limited value. Stakeholders judge an organization by what it does. This is why the second element of the foundation focuses on evidence. Leaders must articulate the behaviors that prove their values and demonstrate those behaviors across every surface.

These behaviors become proof points. They validate what the organization says. They build credibility in environments where skepticism is high and patience is low. Proof points give stakeholders something they can hold on to in moments of uncertainty. They also serve as assets for the broader ecosystem, because they are the examples that get quoted, shared, and reused.

In an omnichannel world, proof points matter more than messages. They travel farther. They carry more weight. They allow the brand to participate in a global conversation without relying on slogans. Proof points give the organization a reputation that is earned rather than declared.

AI-AWARE

Reputation now lives inside search engines, automated summaries, and the large language models that people rely on for quick answers. Leaders must assume that AI is interpreting their organization long before a customer, reporter, regulator, or community member arrives at any official channel. For this reason, the foundation must include an AI-aware footprint. This means understanding that AI systems gather information from the open world, assemble patterns, and generate conclusions based on what they find, not on what the organization wishes were true.

An AI-aware footprint recognizes that organizations no longer control the path through which people learn about them.

When someone asks a system who you are, the model will not check your mission statement or wait for a press release. It will draw from visible signals, public content, earned stories, and the proof points available in the digital ecosystem. If those signals are thin, inconsistent, out of date, or overwhelmed by external narratives, the AI-generated interpretation will reflect that reality.

This is why organizations must treat AI as a reputational surface even if they do not fully understand how AI works. The mechanics of the technology are less important than its influence. Language models do not need permission to evaluate the brand. They are already doing it. They summarize, infer, and repeat what the world appears to believe. For leaders, the responsibility is not to master the architecture of the models but to ensure that credible, accurate material exists in the environment for those models to learn from.

An AI-aware foundation prioritizes clarity, consistency, and discoverability. It ensures that the most reliable version of the narrative is present, visible, and reinforced across channels. It does not require constant output or excessive volume. It requires disciplined signals that reflect reality and support the organization's long-term storyline. When AI systems search for meaning, they should find the organization's true identity, not a distorted echo shaped by neglect.

In this sense, being AI-aware is no longer optional. It is part of modern reputation stewardship. The organization does not need to understand every detail of how AI systems operate. It only needs to understand that those systems now play a decisive role in shaping how people perceive and discuss the brand. Awareness of that influence, and preparation for it, is what turns AI from a risk into a reputational safeguard.

INTERNAL ALIGNMENT

Reputation begins internally. Employees carry the story. Operational systems reinforce or contradict it. Decision-making processes reflect it every day. A foundation cannot exist only in external messaging. It must inform how people inside the organization understand their purpose and their role in sustaining it.

Internal alignment is the point at which reputation becomes real. It shows up in how teams talk about the brand, how they respond to challenges, how they support customers, and how they execute strategy. When internal alignment is weak, even the strongest external story begins to fracture. When internal alignment is strong, the entire organization becomes a coherent expression of the brand.

Internal alignment also accelerates decision-making. When people share an understanding of the foundation, they can act with confidence in unfamiliar situations. They know what to protect and what to reinforce. They also know which decisions will support the long-term reputation and which will undermine it.

THE PRESENT AND FUTURE STORYLINE

A foundation is not a static artifact. It contains the organization's current commitments and future direction. It reflects what the company has done and what it intends to do. This storyline must be clear, honest, and accountable.

The present storyline establishes credibility. The future storyline establishes intention. Together they form the narrative arc that guides the organization through an omnichannel environment. Stakeholders rely on this arc to decide whether the organization is moving in a direction they support. The storyline must appear in every channel, because it shapes expectations. When expectations are clear, organizations gain the benefit of stakeholder patience. When expectations are vague, stakeholders fill the gaps with their own assumptions.

When all five elements are in place, the foundation becomes the reference point for every action and every message. It ensures that the organization can express itself consistently regardless of the channel. It provides simplicity in a world where complexity increases every year. This is the core strength of omnichannel strategy: the ability to express one identity through many forms without losing clarity.

The Omnichannel Surface Is All-Inclusive

In most companies, the word *omnichannel* is associated with marketing. This definition is too limited. Omnichannel reputation work involves every surface where the organization appears and every environment where stakeholders form judgments. It is not a communications grid. It is a map of influence.

The omnichannel universe now includes digital experiences, search results, AI interpretations, social content, shared platforms, earned media, owned publishing, paid advertising, community networks, stakeholder forums, internal channels, customer service interactions, and more. These are not separate streams. They work together, shaping how people understand the organization in both predictable and unpredictable ways.

Some channels provide reach. Others provide depth. Some move quickly. Others create longevity. Each one influences reputation in a different way. Leaders must understand how these channels interact and how meaning shifts as it travels across them. They must also recognize that stakeholders may enter the story at any point. A single comment in a low-traffic forum may shape the narrative for thousands once it is picked up by a search engine or echoed by a trusted voice.

Effective omnichannel leadership requires awareness of this ecosystem and the discipline to maintain coherence within it. It requires leaders to think beyond individual campaigns and focus on the patterns that shape perception over time. It also requires investment in the channels that matter most to the organization's specific audience. No company needs to be everywhere, but every company must know where its narrative is formed.

Steering the System in Real Time

A system of this scale needs structure. That structure comes from a cross-functional body that monitors intelligence, interprets risks, identifies opportunities, and steers the organization's response. This group can be described as the Reputation Council.

The council is not an emergency team waiting for crises. It is an always-on leadership function that anticipates issues and adjusts the organization's posture. It has three responsibilities: to establish, to protect, and to propel the organization's reputation.

"To establish" means to reinforce the foundation. This includes creating content that reflects the organization's identity, ensuring that proof points are visible, and maintaining clarity across channels. "To protect" means to monitor vulnerabilities and act quickly when signals indicate a shift in sentiment or risk. "To propel" means to promote the strengths that deserve more attention and to amplify the evidence that supports the long-term reputation story.

The council must have representation from across the enterprise. Communications, marketing, legal, operations, HR, technology, and customer experience each bring essential knowledge. Together they assess what the organization is signaling, how audiences are responding, and where the narrative is trending. The council is both strategic and operational. It thinks ahead while also acting in the present.

One of the most important roles within the council is the individual who understands the mechanics of the channels. This person has practical knowledge of how content moves, how formats differ, how algorithms interpret information, and how speed affects outcomes. Their insight allows the council to act with precision rather than guesswork.

As reputation becomes a primary driver of enterprise value, the need for structured leadership grows. Many organizations are beginning to recognize the value of a senior role dedicated to this work. The emergence of the chief reputation officer (CRO) position reflects this shift. This role brings focus and accountability to a discipline that influences every part of enterprise performance. It signals to the organization that reputation is central to growth, not peripheral.

Community as a Reputational Asset

Community is often misunderstood. It is not a distribution list, a set of followers, or a collection of stakeholders who occasionally react to the brand. Community is a living network. It carries trust and creates meaning. It shapes how messages are interpreted and how narratives stabilize in moments of uncertainty.

Strong communities do more than engage. They defend. They support. They correct misunderstandings before they grow. They reinforce the elements of the foundation that matter most. These communities emerge when organizations build relationships rather than audiences. They grow when people feel aligned with the brand's meaning and connected to its actions.

In an omnichannel environment, community functions as both a channel and an asset. It amplifies strengths and reduces vulnerabilities. It supports the organization's long-term storyline. It provides resilience in moments when external narratives shift. Leaders who cultivate community early build a reputational buffer that becomes invaluable over time.

From Channels to Coherence

Omnichannel strategy is not about mastering the details of every platform. It is about creating a reputation that holds steady as the world shifts around it. When the foundation is clear and the system is aligned, channels become expressions of identity rather than sources of confusion.

The foundation provides stability. The omnichannel system provides reach. The Reputation Council provides guidance. Community provides reinforcement. Together they form an environment where reputation can grow with intention rather than by chance.

Because information moves instantly and interpretation never stops, leaders must understand one simple truth: The story is always being written. The question is whether the organization is participating in the writing or allowing others to do it.

A strong foundation, supported by an aligned omnichannel system, allows leaders to shape outcomes rather than merely respond to them. This is the work of modern reputation leadership. It is not defined by platforms. It is defined by coherence. And coherence is the most powerful reputational asset any organization can build.

TAKEAWAYS

- *Build the foundation first.* Define the identity, behaviors, and proof points that must stay consistent everywhere the brand appears.

- *Make the foundation AI-aware.* Ensure language models and search systems can find accurate, fact-based signals about the organization.

- *Align internally.* Give employees a clear understanding of the foundation so their actions reinforce the external story.
- *Treat every touchpoint as reputational.* Digital channels, earned media, internal systems, and community spaces all shape how stakeholders judge the brand.
- *Establish a Reputation Council.* Create a cross-functional group that tracks signals and guides how the organization establishes, protects, and propels its reputation.
- *Strengthen community networks.* Invest in relationships that create trust and support the organization when narratives shift.
- *Test the system regularly.* Run drills to confirm that messages can move through all channels with speed, clarity, and consistency.
- *Lead for coherence.* Prioritize clarity and alignment across the organization so the reputation remains steady as conditions change.

Chapter 20

IF YOU CAN'T WIN ATTENTION, YOU CAN'T WIN REPUTATION

Attention is not some free-floating magical element or abstract psychological phenomenon. Attention is a physical property of life. It's constrained by our cognitive abilities, which are determined by our physiology. Our attention spans seem shorter these days because we're constantly bombarded with more information than we can absorb, process, and make sense of.

In today's complex media environment, attention is a scarce resource. Smartphones, packed with apps, alerts, streams, and endless feeds, create an unrelenting flow of content that easily overwhelms our cognitive capacity.[1] That's why our attention spans seem shorter than they did in the past. Our brains cannot keep up; they are overstimulated and outmatched. Our continuous state of overstimulation also goes a long way toward explaining the

TL;DR phenomenon, short for "too long; didn't read," which has become the excuse du jour for not reading anything longer than a couple of paragraphs.[2]

It's imperative for all of us in the reputation management field to recognize that a large share of the audience will not read content in textual form. Instead, they prefer short bursts of information or audio they can listen to while doing something else. One of the reasons TikTok videos and podcasts are so popular is that our overstimulated brains can no longer cope with traditional forms of media, which take too long to consume and require too much attention.

Teachers tell me they see immediate improvements in the attitudes and responsiveness of students when they're asked to put away their mobile phones. Several states are considering legislation that would enable school districts to ban mobile phones from classrooms, which I think would be a step in the right direction.

Automating Fear, Rage, and Anger

It's not just attention that's under assault; it's the entire information environment. Smartphones flooded our focus; now AI is overwhelming our ability to separate truth from distortion, signal from noise. With off-the-shelf tools, a bad actor can launch a reputational crisis from their living room with fake news, social posts, and even deepfakes, all within a span of minutes.

Trolling and rage-baiting have entered a new phase. AI fine-tunes language for maximum provocation, generates replies and headlines, and exploits emotional triggers at scale. These messages spread not because they're accurate, but because they spark outrage. Once they go viral, they can damage reputations, trigger boycotts, or even sink stock prices before the truth has a chance to catch up.

And then there are incendiary tweets. A single high-profile post—authored or AI-assisted—can dominate headlines, derail messaging, and set off news cycles no PR team can control. If it comes from a celebrity CEO, insider, or political influencer, the impact can be staggering. AI only amplifies the risk by testing emotional resonance and timing releases for maximum disruption.

AI isn't another tool in the communications tool kit; it's an accelerant, a megaphone, and, in the wrong hands, a flamethrower. Managing reputation in this environment means thinking less like traditional communicators and more like digital strategists in a live-fire zone.

The Shelf Life of Reputation

Reputation is fleeting—especially now. Public interest shifts with dizzying speed. Artists and celebrities who once seemed omnipresent can vanish from the conversation almost overnight. In his 2025 essay "What Happened to the Celebrities?" critic Ted Gioia observes that today's entertainment culture is no longer built on stars but built on micro-moments and viral fragments. The center no longer holds because, increasingly, there is no center, just a relentless churn of content and attention. Companies such as Nike and Disney have discovered that massive investments in celebrities and celebrity brands no longer deliver the expected returns.[3]

This shift is most visible in music, where virality is both the path to fame and the reason it fades so quickly. Data journalist Daniel Parris notes that music stardom now burns bright and fast, with fewer artists achieving lasting recognition. In today's saturated media economy, it's not enough to break through once; you must break through repeatedly or be forgotten.[4]

The new reality of fame can also be cruel. Commentator Abby Roth observes that female pop stars in particular face brutally short "shelf lives," pressured to constantly reinvent while punished for changing too much. Fame becomes a precarious balancing act between relevance and respectability, and visibility and exhaustion.[5]

These dynamics have profound implications for reputation management. A brand or public figure might dominate the conversation today and be forgotten, or canceled, by next quarter. The rise of micro-trends, fleeting aesthetic waves amplified by TikTok and Instagram, has trained audiences to crave the new-new thing.[6] A fashion trend that's "in" one week can become passé the next.[7]

You may be tempted to think, "Oh sure, but this whole micro-trend thing applies mainly to pop music, teen fashion, and caffeinated beverages." But you would be wrong. It's indisputable that micro-trends now have macro impacts on public perception, consumer behavior, and brand reputation. That's because today's trends don't trickle down; they erupt, go viral, and burn out. The same logic now governs cultural attention across every sector.

This creates a paradox: The more visible you are, the more vulnerable you become to rapid shifts in taste and sentiment. Reputation managers today must accept that the same tools used to amplify a message can just as easily extinguish it. Every algorithmically enhanced surge of visibility carries the risk of a backlash. Every hashtag that lifts a brand can just as easily be flipped into something mocking, ironic, or hostile. Glory is now conditional—and crowdsourced.

What does that mean for reputation strategy? It means you build resilience, not permanence. You don't count on attention spans—you adapt to them. You create modular narratives that evolve with the moment. You invest in credibility, not just virality. And you don't chase relevance at the cost of trust. Because in the end, relevance without trust is a short ride to nowhere.

That's the new ground game. Not just monitoring headlines but anticipating cultural shifts. Not just managing crisis but managing momentum. Because when fame is fleeting, reputational gravity pulls hard. Only those with deep roots in authenticity will achieve lasting success.

TAKEAWAYS

- *Recognize* attention as finite; every message competes in a crowded, fragmented marketplace.
- *Prioritize* clarity and meaning over volume; noise erodes credibility.

- *Design* communication that earns attention by aligning with values and delivering relevance.
- *Protect* audiences from fatigue; discipline in messaging sustains trust.
- *Treat* attention as reputational currency; use it sparingly, strategically, and with intent.

Chapter 21

THE ALGORITHM IS WATCHING: WHY CONSISTENCY BUILDS CREDIBILITY

Reputation isn't defined by a single campaign or headline moment; it's a continuous cycle of showing up. In today's attention economy, where competitors jostle for mindshare by the hour, the velocity of reputation-building has accelerated. A two-week absence from customer engagement can feel like an eternity. Is it a deliberate pause, building suspense before a big launch, or has something bad happened? The battle for relevance now plays out in feeds and platforms where expectations shift constantly. Reputation equity should be managed like a high-frequency account, with regular contributions of meaningful content, reliable product performance, and authentic interactions. Above all, however, a brand's reputation strategy must be consistent and continuous.

I've seen firsthand how reputation equity has to be nurtured continuously in today's markets. And it's not just human audiences making judgments anymore. Algorithms have become silent stakeholders in every brand's reputation. Consequently, mastering algorithmic fluency is now a strategic requirement for leaders. In the article "Branding in the Age of Algorithms: Why Algorithmic Fluency Is the New Brand Superpower," Jeanine Moss makes the case that brand equity today is shaped not only by human trust but also by how machines interpret our signals.[1]

For decades, brand building was about shaping human perception. Campaigns, visuals, and narratives were designed to move people emotionally and inspire loyalty. That work is still essential, Moss argues, but an entirely new layer has emerged between brands and their audiences: algorithms. Search engines, social feeds, recommendation systems, and AI assistants now decide whether our stories are seen, heard, or ignored. In her words, reputation today is "both a human truth and a machine calculation."[2]

She describes this dual challenge as "algorithmic fluency"—the ability to design a brand that speaks fluently to both people and platforms.[3] Algorithms don't feel emotion, but they measure signals: backlinks, dwell time, reviews, tags, engagement velocity, structured data, and sentiment. Each of these machine-readable inputs influences whether a brand is elevated or buried. Brands fluent in these signals gain discoverability, scale personalization, and maintain consistency across fragmented digital landscapes.

Moss outlines three shifts in mindset that define algorithmic fluency:

1. *Design for discovery, not just delivery.* A compelling brand story is meaningless if it isn't surfaced. Algorithms reward

content that is structured, explicit, and interconnected. Clarity, topic clustering, and engagement velocity all help platforms recognize relevance. Consistency across publishing reinforces reliability.

2. *Treat algorithms as stakeholders.* Just as we shape messages for customers or investors, brands must now shape signals for platforms. Each algorithm has values: Search engines reward authority and clarity; social platforms reward velocity of engagement; recommendation engines reward retention; and AI assistants reward structured, high-quality sources. Reputation equity here means building trust not just with people but with the systems mediating their attention.

3. *Balance precision with emotion.* Machines may determine reach, but humans decide resonance. Precision ensures content is machine-readable—clear language, structured metadata, consistent themes—while emotion ensures that when content surfaces, it connects. Storytelling, tone, design, and empathy are what transform visibility into loyalty.[4]

Ultimately, Moss leaves us with a defining question: Is your brand more what you say it is, or what the algorithm decides it is? That question captures the modern reality of reputation. Brand equity is no longer built only on deposits of human trust; it also depends on how clearly and consistently we send signals that machines can parse and amplify. The tension becomes obvious when brands discover that the audience they think they're reaching isn't the one actually engaging. Algorithms often "reveal" them to entirely different groups—younger, more global, or more niche than expected.

For leaders thinking about reputation equity, Moss's framework is a reminder that the audience isn't only human anymore. It is now composed of communities of people and lines of code.

TAKEAWAYS

- *Publish* consistently across channels; gaps in presence raise suspicion.
- *Design* content for discovery, not just delivery; structure signals so algorithms elevate your brand.
- *Treat* algorithms as active partners in reputation. Study what each platform's algorithm rewards, decode its preferences, and adapt your content inputs to earn visibility and trust. Remember that no single approach works across all platforms.
- *Balance* machine precision with human resonance: clarity for platforms, emotion for people.
- *Sustain* reputational velocity by making regular, meaningful deposits of content, performance, and interaction.

Part IV

THEORY AND FRAMEWORKS

Chapter 22

THE HUMAN CODE BEHIND REPUTATION: WIRED TO WATCH, BUILT TO JUDGE

Reputation has always been a cornerstone of human interaction, influencing decisions from choosing friends to forming communities. The digital age has put a new spin on reputation, yet its significance is deeply rooted in our evolutionary past. Long ago—thousands of years before hashtags, tweets, and TikTok videos were even imagined, much less invented—reputation was already doing heavy lifting in human society, playing a major role in helping our ancestors survive, form alliances, and avoid getting thrown out of the tribe.

The more you look into the roots of reputation, the more you realize how it still depends on instincts that were shaped in the earliest days of cooperation and interdependency of social beings, even before us humans. Frankly, the idea that all of us are hardwired with the ability to evaluate reputation is a scary notion. But there's no getting around it, so let's just accept that we are imbued with this superpower and learn how to use it!

In his Substack publication *Conspicuous Cognition*, Dan Williams introduces the idea of "strategic paranoia," the notion that being a little jumpy can be smart, even when it seems irrational. Even irrationality itself can prove valuable in the right circumstances. "One of the central lessons of game theory is that behaviors that would be irrational if one were alone on a desert island can advance one's strategic interests when interacting with others," he writes.[1]

An inherent vigilance toward potential threats, even to the point of paranoia, can serve as a deterrent against exploitation. In other words, if people think you're watching closely and ready to call out any bad behavior, they're less likely to cross you, Williams explains. In a reputation strategy context, hypervigilance serves as a powerful early-warning system.[2] This is further backed by decades of social studies. Multiple experiments show that individuals are significantly more likely to act ethically, recycle, donate, or conform to social norms when they feel they are being watched, even by something as simple as a pair of eyes printed on a poster. This phenomenon is sometimes called the "watching-eye effect."[3] It suggests that perceived surveillance nudges people toward better behavior—not necessarily because of moral conviction, but because of the reputational risk of being seen doing otherwise. This doesn't mean threatening people with exposure, but rather creating a context where transparency is assumed and accountability is likely.

Never underestimate the "judgy-ness" of human nature. "We're not just social; we're *ultra*-social. We're completely dependent on intricate and intense forms of cooperation to achieve even the most basic requirements of survival. This cooperation occurs within large, complex social networks organized around norms, reputations, gossip, and status games in which people compete to win respect, admiration, and social influence," Williams writes.[4]

Authors and visionary thinkers such as Peter Kropotkin, Matt Ridley, and Richard Dawkins have also contributed to my perspectives on the evolutionary underpinnings of reputation. In *Mutual Aid*, Kropotkin makes the case that it wasn't just competition that shaped evolution; it was cooperation. He noticed that animals that supported each other often had better survival odds than those that fought solo. Those who appeared healthier, smarter, or stronger had better chances of mating, obtaining resources, and becoming leaders. And the same goes for humans. Communities that trusted each other and pooled resources thrived. If your reputation made you someone others could rely on, your chances of sticking around went way up.[5]

Ridley picks up this thread in *The Origins of Virtue*. He argues that morality—what we think of today as being "a good person"—evolved as a strategy for living in groups. Reciprocal altruism is the name of the game: You scratch my back now, and I'll scratch yours later. That only works if people believe you'll keep your end of the deal. Which is where reputation comes in. If you're seen as someone who doesn't return favors or breaks trust, the system falls apart. But if you're known as dependable? You get invited back, again and again.[6]

In *The Selfish Gene*, Dawkins reframes everything through the lens of gene survival—basically, your behavior helps your genes replicate. That includes doing things that improve your social standing, growth potential, and long-term stability. If keeping a good name gave you an edge, your genes were all for it. In that sense, reputation isn't fluff. It's fitness.[7]

What does all this mean for businesses today? It means that managing your reputation isn't merely a matter of managing superficial appearances. It's about being seen as trustworthy, aware, plugged in, and dependable. Managing reputation means showing your team, your customers, and your critics that you *get* what's at stake. And that sometimes means anticipating trouble before it arrives.

Williams's concept of strategic paranoia seems especially relevant today. If you're a brand, you don't just worry about what you say—you also imagine how it might be clipped, memed, or interpreted in ways that could go viral. In that kind of environment, a little healthy paranoia goes a long way. It's not about living in fear. It's about being prepared and being able to improvise.

Don't be afraid to war-game potential crises. Scan your own culture for red flags and ask, "If I weren't me, what would I find problematic about this?"

TAKEAWAYS

- *Recognize* that reputational instincts are evolutionary—use them to your advantage.
- *Leverage* trust, reciprocity, and inclusion as timeless reputation drivers.
- *Frame* reputation strategy in terms of belonging; exclusion damages credibility.

- *Anticipate* reputational attacks—vigilance is preparation, not paranoia.
- *Design* modern systems that respect ancient instincts for fairness and status.

Chapter 23

BUILT TO BELONG: HOW COMMUNITY SHAPES REPUTATION

Reputation equity carries an emotional dimension. Given that brand interactions are deeply personalized—filtered through phones, apps, and social feeds—reputation doesn't just signal trust; it signals belonging. When people feel a sense of belonging, they treat the brand less like a transaction and more like a relationship.

This emotional bond explains why consumers with a strong connection to a brand are more forgiving of mistakes. A delayed shipment, a flawed product, or an awkward campaign doesn't necessarily destroy the relationship; it's interpreted through the broader lens of trust that's already been earned. In effect, reputation equity gives brands a margin of grace.

Just as important, the personal nature of the connection creates space for experimentation. Customers who feel attached to a brand are not only more open to new products or services; they're eager to participate in shaping them. This is the essence of cocreation—where audiences offer feedback, launch campaigns, or even build communities around the brand's future direction.

In this way, reputation becomes more than credibility. It's a shared narrative. The brand tells its story, and its customers help write the next chapter. That's why reputation equity is both durable and dynamic: It can't be manufactured overnight, but once earned, it becomes a living resource that fuels collaboration, innovation, and growth.

When Emotional Connection Becomes Market Power

Reputation equity can inspire levels of engagement and loyalty that are strong enough to influence business decisions. Here are recent examples of how emotional bonds translate into market power:

- *LEGO Ideas:* Fans design and vote on sets, many of which become official products.
- *Netflix fan campaigns:* Movements have resurrected shows like *Lucifer* and *Arrested Development.*
- *Coca-Cola's "New Coke" reversal:* Consumer backlash forced the return of the classic formula in the 1980s.
- *Fenty Beauty:* Community demand for inclusive shades reshaped the cosmetics industry.

- *Heritage snack revivals:* Fan pressure revived products like Twinkies and Crystal Pepsi.

These cases highlight why emotional connection isn't just a soft benefit; it's a strategic resource that strengthens reputation equity and fuels future growth.

Yes, It's Personal

One of the biggest shifts in reputation today is how personal it feels. Ten or twenty years ago, brands were distant entities. You'd catch their message in a TV spot, a billboard, or maybe a magazine ad. It was transactional, not relational. Today, it's different. Because we interact with content on phones, in feeds, and in real time, we feel as if we actually "know" the brands we let into our lives. Algorithms don't replace the age-old mechanism of relatability, but they do mediate it, sometimes connecting brands to unexpected audiences, sometimes distorting who the "relatable self" actually is.

That sense of familiarity cuts both ways. When a brand consistently delivers, I don't just see it as reliable; I see it as part of my daily circle. I forgive mistakes the way I'd forgive a friend, because the reputation they've earned buys them that latitude. On the other hand, when a brand's reputation is shaky, the connection feels more like meeting someone you can't quite trust. You hold back. You keep them at a distance.

This is why reputation equity matters so much. It shapes not only market opportunity but also the depth of personal connection.

In many ways, reputation is the social currency that determines whether people invite a brand into their personal lives.

That sense of attachment often mirrors the dynamics of fandom. Audiences who follow a character season after season develop a one-sided familiarity that can even shape storylines: Fan campaigns have resurrected canceled shows, kept characters alive, and pushed studios to greenlight sequels. The same patterns appear in business. Communities keep products alive long after companies stop backing them. Think of buyers who clamor for discontinued snacks, rally around heritage brands, or push for more inclusive skincare lines until companies respond. Here, reputation functions less like advertising and more like collective memory and advocacy, with loyalty translating into market pressure.

A Platform for Expansion

Linking reputation to growth and market expansion means treating equity as both shield and springboard. The shield protects a brand when challenges arise—a faulty product, a negative headline, or a shifting regulatory landscape. With equity in reserve, a company earns the benefit of the doubt, buying time and goodwill while it corrects course. Without that shield, even small mistakes can feel catastrophic, as customers and stakeholders assume the worst.

The springboard, on the other hand, is what launches a brand into new spaces. Reputation equity creates confidence among consumers to try a new product, among partners to join a venture, and among regulators to allow entry into sensitive markets. It gives leaders permission to take risks, knowing that trust provides a softer landing if the leap doesn't go perfectly.

Thinking of reputation equity in this dual role clarifies why it's so powerful. Reputation isn't just defense or offense, protection or propulsion. It's both, working together. A shield without a springboard leads to caution and stagnation. A springboard without a shield leads to overreach and collapse. The brands that thrive are those that cultivate both dimensions of equity; they are strong enough to weather storms and bold enough to leap into the future.

Reputation equity determines whether customers carry over to the next product, whether regulators see a brand as a partner or a risk, and whether employees advocate for its mission in public. In a competitive landscape defined by speed, personalization, and transparency, managing reputation equity is no longer optional. It is the growth strategy.

TAKEAWAYS

- *Cultivate* emotional bonds that transform customers into advocates who forgive mistakes.
- *Invite* audiences to cocreate—through feedback, campaigns, and community-building initiatives.
- *Translate* fandom energy into innovation; listen to what your most passionate supporters demand.

- *Recognize* that reputation equity buys grace—use it to test bold ideas.
- *Leverage* emotional connection as market power; collective passion can reverse decisions, revive products, or force industry change.

Chapter 24

BUILDING REPUTATION IN A WORLD WITHOUT PRIVACY

Three thousand years ago, Socrates said, "Know thyself." I would never argue with Socrates, but I would respectfully add, "And know how other people perceive you."

Your reputation reflects how the world sees you. Before the internet, social media, smartphones, and omnipresent surveillance became part of daily living, it was possible to separate our private selves from our public personas. Today, privacy is a sentimental fantasy. If you're a global corporation or a government agency, you might as well forget about trying to keep secrets. You're at the mercy of any system administrator with a thumb drive. Just ask Edward Snowden how easy it is to steal classified information!

You don't need access to secrets to cause embarrassment or to cast doubt on a brand's integrity. An internet search can reveal which brands are paying subminimum wages to their workers or using child labor to make the sneakers you're wearing. With AI tools like ChatGPT, Gemini, and Claude at your disposal, it's easy to create detailed lists of brands that harbor potentially embarrassing "secrets" they would prefer to downplay or ignore. Furthermore, it's easier than ever to create smear campaigns and content that isn't real and to play with the fact that more than half the population is overconfident in their ability to spot AI-generated content. And very few people will actively fact-check the information that is presented to them.

Bad actors will have a difficult time disrupting a credible brand with an established reputation, while a bad personal experience will affect a brand for a very long time.

We live in a world of radical transparency. Get used to it because it's not going away anytime soon. But let's begin by accepting the reality of our situation. We live in a panopticon. It's a scary concept originally proposed by the philosopher Jeremy Bentham, who described it as a circular prison where a guard could observe prisoners without them knowing when they were being observed. Unlike the prisoners in Bentham's panopticon, who were only observed by a single guard, we must assume that we're being observed all the time by an unknown number of others.

TAKEAWAYS

- *Acknowledge* radical transparency; assume every action will be observed and shared.
- *Audit* vulnerabilities before they're exposed by others.
- *Prepare* for misinformation; train teams to verify, respond, and correct quickly.

- *Strengthen* your reputation so it resists manipulation and hostile campaigns.
- *Operate* as if under constant observation; integrity is your only sustainable shield.

Chapter 25

REPUTATION ISN'T TOLD—IT'S CREATED LAYER BY LAYER

Communication modalities have evolved wildly over time, from cave paintings and pictographs to rapid-fire texting and emojis. In the past six thousand years, we've gone from stone tablets to fully immersive virtual reality multiple-player games.

Just as facial expressions and body language add emotional nuance to real-life conversations, emojis and GIFs serve as tone indicators in digital exchanges. As communication speeds up, so does the need for shortcuts, making it essential to balance speed with authenticity, as form continues to evolve alongside function. To communicate effectively, brands must layer context through thoughtful visuals, design choices, and timely responses—while staying attuned to emerging signals like voice notes, AR interactions, and, most important, how messages are received as audiences move fluidly across platforms and formats.

It's also worth considering how the Aristotelian concept of the "golden mean" (finding balance between extremes) also applies to modern reputation strategy. While vigilance is crucial, there's a fine line between being appropriately cautious and overly paranoid. Excessive wariness can lead to missed opportunities and a culture of fear, while insufficient caution may result in reputational blind spots. Striking the right balance ensures that organizations remain alert to potential threats without stifling innovation or responsiveness.

This balanced approach is particularly relevant in today's fast-paced digital landscape, where public perception can shift rapidly. By embracing a "middle way," businesses can navigate the complexities of reputation management more effectively, maintaining trust and credibility without succumbing to the pitfalls of either extreme vigilance or complacency.[1]

For brands, it's important to align across all channels and to prioritize which channels are actually critical to reputation strategy. The future will be shaped by brands that can rebuild trust, not by being perfect but by being principled and consistent.

Here's an idea worth considering: Instead of looking at reputation strategy as a battle or competitive debate, imagine it as a collaborative discussion. Battles are zero-sum contests that have to be won. When we're dealing with reputation strategy, however, the "winner takes all" approach can backfire. It signals defensiveness and hidden intentions.

Remember, our minds and instincts have been honed by evolution to spot signs of dishonesty and to interpret them as indications of weakness. A discussion mindset, on the other hand, values inquiry, openness, and the ability to engage constructively, signaling confidence and self-assurance—key traits that are essential for building reputational success.

Signaling Credibility in the Age of AI

Amid the clutter of avatars, algorithmic influencers, and AI-generated content, the ability to signal credibility has become both harder and more valuable. The key is not to be flawless, but to be legible and consistent—because inconsistency is what triggers doubt in both humans and machines.

What makes this moment in time so unique is the emergence of what might be called "synthetic reputation," a blend of human perception and machine amplification. As we step out of the caves and into the metaverse, the rules of reputation haven't disappeared. In an age of digital agents, not all reputation is earned; some is synthesized.

If the ancient brain was built to gossip around a campfire, today's mind is trained to scan feeds, decode subtext, and adjust its public face in milliseconds. Your trust score is now partly shaped by how well your digital self performs: what gets picked up by algorithms, who validates your content, and how your signals are interpreted across different platforms.

From Stack Overflow moderators debating the line between earned and inflated scores to AI systems combining witness reports with trust metrics, the rise of synthetic reputation is reshaping what it means to be credible and what it means to navigate trust at scale.[2]

Scholars remind us that gossip wasn't just idle talk—it has always served as reputation currency, enforcing norms and group membership. In a way, today's retweets, likes, and comments are just a modern form of this same ancient practice. And just as gossip once determined whether you'd be trusted with a hunt or burnt at the stake, your digital footprint now influences whether you're trusted with a partnership, a vote, or a job.

Despite the scale and speed of modern communications, the ancient insight from Plato still holds: that public perception is ultimately a dialogue between *who we are*, *who we appear to be*, and *who others need us to be*. Today, the tension between those three identities plays out not in the agora but on platforms like TikTok or LinkedIn. These are more than records of single important moments; they're living, evolving reputation systems. Similarly, the brand that once polished quarterly press releases now needs to manage a 24/7 loop of micro-reputational feedback from all angles.

To lead reputationally in this era is about knowing how to stand in the spotlight, reflect it, and sometimes, redirect it. Leaders must learn to not just read the room, but to listen to the frequency behind the signal. The best players are the most consistent, the most adaptive, and the most self-aware.

Anonymity as a Survival Strategy

Our desires to be seen, understood, and trusted have never disappeared. Yet more of our life experiences are now occurring in digital spaces. We have evolved into semi-digital beings; the data that defines our digital identities now defines us. Everything we do in the digital space is captured and stored. Thanks to ubiquitous surveillance cameras, listening devices, and location detection systems, many of our everyday activities in the "real world" are also captured and translated into data. And that data can be difficult to erase. For all practical purposes, it is beyond the control of most people.

This raises a difficult question: What does reputation strategy look like in a world where a blend of social data is the default measure of our perceived value? Ironically, one answer lies in the intentional use of anonymity, a strategy as old as storytelling itself. Long before social media handles were invented, writers like Mary Ann Evans (George Eliot), François-Marie Arouet (Voltaire), and Samuel Langhorne Clemens (Mark Twain) created noms de plume to shield and protect themselves while publishing controversial, and sometimes incendiary, ideas.

Of course, anonymity is not confined to literary authors alone; today, it's fully entwined and wired into the culture of digital life. In gaming communities, most players go by screen names that reveal practically nothing about their real-world identities. This trend isn't limited to games. On platforms like Instagram, TikTok, Discord, and Reddit, people are subtly encouraged to create usernames that express identity without confirming it. Anonymity and aliases have become a layer of performance: one that lets individuals curate their vibe, control their narrative, or simply exist without being fully exposed.[3]

Enter Banksy, the graffiti artist who has built a global brand while remaining anonymous. In a world obsessed with personal branding and visibility, anonymity might seem like a liability, but for some, it's a masterstroke. Artists like Banksy and others have turned their creative aliases into brands, leveraging their anonymity to achieve a higher level of narrative control and to inspire an aura of mystery. Musical artists like Sia or Melanie Martinez and others may also choose to use a stage persona or even hide their faces to put the focus on their art and performance instead of their personalities.

Glancing into the Future

Even after millennia of change, refinement, and reinvention, the norms, narratives, and tools surrounding reputation formation remain unsettled. The processes we use to create, measure, repair, and protect our reputations are in flux; they're shaped and then reshaped by cultural shifts, advances in technology, and a seemingly endless parade of anxiety-provoking uncertainties around finance, trade, politics, climate change, healthcare, education, career ascent, family life, and a host of other challenges. In other words, the processes of reputation formation are continually evolving. For reputation professionals, this means shifting from reactive brand protection to proactive reputation design.

The present and the future demand that we become cartographers of perception—mapping emerging norms, decoding cultural cues, and identifying the invisible dynamics shaping how we are seen and perceived by others.

Most of all, we need to convey that behind the brands we represent, there are real humans trying to do the right thing. I refuse to believe that millions of years of evolution have brought us to a point where we will be overwhelmed by the technologies we've created. The situations we find ourselves in today may be daunting, but they are far from insurmountable. Our role as reputation strategists is to determine the most effective ways to leverage the tools at our disposal and to keep the campfires burning.

TAKEAWAYS

- *Map* the layers of context—personal, cultural, industry, global—that shape meaning.
- *Craft* messages that resonate across multiple layers without losing coherence.
- *Test* narratives with diverse audiences to ensure relevance and credibility.
- *Anchor* every action in a broader story that connects to values.
- *Remember:* context turns isolated actions into lasting reputation.

Chapter 26

REPUTATION IS WHAT FANS MEME ABOUT YOU

Under the right circumstances, relationships between brands, fans, and media platforms can become mutually reinforcing. One of my favorite examples of how this happens is *Arcane*, the animated Emmy Award–winning Netflix series based on characters and lore from *League of Legends*, a popular online multiplayer game developed by Riot Games.[1]

But *Arcane* wasn't just another streaming series—it triggered a cultural cascade. By leaning into steampunk aesthetics, alt-rock emotion, and layered characters like Jinx, *Arcane* reached far beyond the gaming community. Suddenly, fans who had never touched a game controller were drawing fan art, cosplaying at cons, and cutting TikToks layered with meaning. These weren't just signs of appreciation; they were acts of affiliation. *Arcane* had become a bridge into new audience segments and creative subcultures.[2]

Welcome to the world of fandoms: self-organizing, emotionally invested, fiercely creative communities that are reshaping how reputation works in modern markets. Fandoms aren't merely groups of customers or social media followers. They are culturally bonded networks that speak their own symbolic languages, often through memes, iconography, and deep-cut references that don't require explanation for insiders. You don't have to be rich, glamorous, or powerful to join a fandom. But you have to understand its unique language and key symbols.

And there need to be touchpoints, which are the *emotional triggers* and *cultural anchors* that build identity, loyalty, and community around a fandom. Touchpoints are recognizable, repeatable, and emotionally resonant experiences or symbols that invite participation and create shared meaning within a fandom. They can be visual (e.g., a logo or character design), auditory (theme music), narrative (key story arcs or catchphrases), or even tactile (merchandise, cosplay materials).

Touchpoints help transform passive consumers into active members of a cultural tribe. They work because they tap into the psychological principles of ritualization and associative memory. Best of all, from a reputational standpoint, touchpoints offer brands a legitimate way to influence fandoms associated with their products.

Think of Taylor Swift fans decoding Easter eggs hidden across her albums or sneakerheads awaiting each new Nike drop with the same reverence others reserve for holidays. Importantly, touchpoints have a cumulative effect. A toddler might demand all things Peppa Pig, just as a teen might grow into anime, K-pop, or Marvel fandoms.

And yes, Harley-Davidson riders also form a fandom that overlaps with other affiliations—like Hard Rock Café, vintage Americana, and Route 66. Even luxury brands are tapping into this. For example, Gucci collaborated with Harry Styles to reach younger, fashion-fluid fans who may have first encountered the brand in video games such as *The Sims*, *Animal Crossing*, or *Roblox*.

Psychology studies show that our brains react to and sense connections with media personalities and fictional characters much like they do with real social relationships. Some call this phenomenon "parasocial engagement." Although parasocial connections and character identifications are sometimes stigmatized for being one-sided, they can support personal growth and social learning, especially when fans interact in communities.[3] Their intensity and effects, however, will vary based on individual traits like attachment style and cultural context.

Many fans continue to follow bands, artists, and shows from their formative years. As nostalgia cycles accelerate, fandom touchpoints often reemerge in new forms: think *Pokémon Go*, the Barbie movie, or any remastered classic. This nostalgia is not regression; it's a reactivation of earlier symbolic touchpoints that now serve new purposes. They become cultural shorthand, allowing brands to signal relevance, tribe alignment, and emotional credibility.

Each initiative is less about the product or the story and more about entering the fans' emotional ecosystems. They help fans feel they are part of something bigger.[4]

Here are some examples of fandom touchpoints:

1. *The Sorting Hat in Harry Potter.* The interactive question of "Which house are you?" is a touchpoint that fans still use to identify with the Hogwarts universe, creating personality-based engagement across generations and media formats.

2. *Jinx's blue hair and graffiti from* Arcane *(*League of Legends*)*. The iconography of Jinx's character (her twin braids, chaotic energy, and stenciled symbols) became a visual shorthand for the show's tone and attracted fans beyond the gaming community, becoming widely shared online and at fan events.

3. *Baja Blast and Taco Bell.* What began as an exclusive soda became a pop-culture touchpoint for Taco Bell fans. Its cult following turned into memes, limited rereleases, and themed merchandise, all reinforcing emotional loyalty through scarcity and nostalgia.

4. *Pokémon merch.* These aren't just products; they're physical touchpoints for collecting and storytelling, turning childhood memories into adult nostalgia and driving reengagement across generations.

5. *The "May the Force Be with You" catchphrase (*Star Wars*)*. This line has become a cultural and linguistic touchpoint; it's used in tweets, campaigns, graduation speeches, and fandom-specific holidays like May the 4th. It's a meme, mantra, and handshake all in one.

Why Touchpoints Matter in Reputation Strategy

Touchpoints enable reputational reach beyond traditional brand messaging. They are:

- *Low-friction entry points* to a brand's world

- *Emotionally sticky* (they stay in your memory and are fun to share)
- *Decentralized* (fans take ownership of the symbols and use them in new contexts, expanding the cultural footprint)

When managed wisely, they create self-sustaining loops of engagement that improve brand equity. But poorly executed or inauthentic touchpoints can create confusion, backlash, or disengagement.[5]

KitKat: The Perfect Marriage of Culture, Fandom, and Brand

There is a well-established KitKat fandom in Japan, and it's a fascinating example of how a global brand adapted to a local culture so effectively that it developed an almost cultlike following. The name "KitKat" sounds similar to the Japanese phrase "kitto katsu" (きっと勝つ), which means "you will surely win." This serendipitous pun made KitKats popular as good-luck gifts, especially for students preparing for exams.

Over time, Nestlé Japan embraced and amplified this cultural link by introducing limited-edition regional and seasonal flavors (such as wasabi, sake, purple sweet potato, and red bean sandwich), which further fueled fan enthusiasm and collectability. KitKats have become a staple of Japan's gifting culture and are often sold in elegant boxes suitable for *omiyage* (souvenirs), reinforcing their use as tokens of goodwill and appreciation.[6]

Additionally, KitKat has collaborated with local artists, offered customizable packaging, and even launched special mailable versions, making it one of the few candy brands to earn a fandom-like following in Japan.[7]

The result is an organic, deeply rooted fandom that extends across generations and geographies within Japan. KitKat's Japanese marketing strategy exemplifies how brands can become embedded in local culture, allowing fans to cocreate meaning and express identity through the product. The unexpected magnitude of KitKat's success in Japan is a master class in cultural localization. Rather than pushing a single global identity, the brand embraced local meaning, ritual, and consumer behavior, creating a sense of emotional resonance that transformed everyday candy into a symbol of encouragement and care.

Communities, Creators, and Cultural Moments

Reputation used to live in press releases, ad campaigns, and boardroom decisions. Today, it lives in memes, Discord threads, TikTok stitches, fan art, and livestreams you didn't authorize. It's shaped by people who may never buy your product but who will absolutely shape how others see you. That's the shift we're living through.

Technology didn't just speed things up. It shattered the old playbook. We're no longer operating in linear media cycles. We're in a chaotic swirl where narratives remix in real time, and credibility is crowdsourced on platforms that don't care about your brand guidelines.

In this new world, reputation is cocreated, often by strangers with no formal stake in your company—just emotional capital, cultural fluency, and access to audiences you can't reach on your own. Sometimes they elevate you. Sometimes they bury you. And sometimes they make you something you never intended to be.

You don't get to control it, but you *can* influence it. That influence starts with humility, curiosity, and a willingness to see your brand not as the center of the universe, but as a participant in a larger cultural conversation. That's where reputation is really built now: at the edges where culture, tech, and community collide.

This chapter explores how to lead in that environment. Not by tightening your grip—but by becoming more adaptive, more culturally fluent, and more willing to listen to the signals coming from the margins.

Memes are artifacts of fandoms. Not the kind brands try to manufacture with awkward winks and hashtags, but the kind born from fans themselves: authentic, chaotic, emotionally spot-on, and occasionally hilarious. Memes act as the native language of fandom, allowing communities to interpret, remix, and broadcast what a brand or character means to them. When brands try to inject themselves too directly into that space, it rarely ends well. The smarter move is to observe, understand, and, when appropriate, amplify. Because sometimes, a meme speaks louder than a campaign.

But reputation in fandom isn't just shaped by content. It's shaped by conduct. A toxic fandom (one that is marked by hostility, exclusion, or relentless negativity) can damage a brand's image no matter how great the product is. We've seen fan communities turn on creators, attack newcomers, or flood social channels with criticism, creating headlines that overshadow the product itself.

On the flip side, a healthy fandom (one that's inclusive, self-aware, and collaborative) can become a brand's greatest asset. Think of the welcoming energy around certain corners of *Magic: The Gathering* or the whimsical intensity of *Animal Crossing* players during the pandemic. Those fandoms didn't just reflect good products; they reflected values that attracted new players, creators, and even strategic partners.

That's where reputation intersects with strategy. Brands looking to partner with others, whether through collaborations, crossovers, or shared experiences, need to understand how their fandoms behave. A "good fandom neighbor" is one whose cultural footprint invites others in, rather than pushing them away. Successful partnerships, like the crossover *Final Fantasy* × *Magic: The Gathering*, work not just because of brand alignment, but because the fandoms share a love of lore, design, and the creative metagame. When fans see the pairing as mutually enriching, they champion it.

TAKEAWAYS

- *Study* fandom behaviors to understand how they amplify or distort your brand.
- *Engage* with fans authentically; they can create momentum you cannot buy.
- *Design* campaigns that invite cocreation with passionate communities.

- *Protect* against toxic fandom dynamics that erode credibility.
- *Treat* fandom energy as cultural currency that fuels long-term reputation.
- *Accept* uncertainty; reputation now emerges at the edges of control.
- *Experiment* in spaces where culture, tech, and community intersect.
- *Build* adaptability into systems; rigidity is reputational risk.
- *Watch* how narratives remix across platforms and learn from the edges.
- *Prepare* leaders for ambiguity; resilience sustains reputation where certainty cannot.

Chapter 27

RED-TEAM YOUR REPUTATION BEFORE SOMEONE ELSE DOES

Reputation isn't just a communications issue; it's a systems issue. If your internal culture isn't aligned with your external message, your response will be weak and wobbly. If your spokespeople haven't practiced crisis language, it will show. If your values can't withstand scrutiny, the public will test them for you.

When your internal culture and external stories don't match, no amount of spin will make your response credible.

In cybersecurity, there's a concept called "red teaming." It's not new; it's been around in military circles for decades. And it's one of the smartest strategies out there. The idea is simple: Before someone else breaks your system, you break it yourself. You build a team whose whole job is to think like an adversary, find your weak spots, and test your ability to respond. You stress-test your own security, so when a real threat shows up, it's not your first rodeo. Now imagine if we did that with reputation.

Reputation is the soft underbelly of every modern brand. One leaked memo, one bad headline, one off-message executive post—and suddenly you're trending for all the wrong reasons. It's not a matter of *if*; it's *when*. Yet most organizations still treat reputation as something you manage when things go wrong. But what if we flipped that? What if, instead of waiting for the storm, you trained for it?

The logic is the same as in cybersecurity: Simulate threats before they're real. Think like your critics. Stress-test your message. Pressure-test your team. Put your people through drills that feel uncomfortably real—because when the crisis hits, it *will* be uncomfortable.

You don't need to be paranoid to benefit from this. Nor do you need to become the brand that mocks itself and excessively uses a mix of vulnerability and humor to get attention.[1] You just need to be honest about how fast things can fall apart. In 2024, Boeing got hammered when the latest round of safety failures turned into a PR nightmare. Their messaging didn't hold. Their internal culture was exposed. And the internet did what the internet does: It lit a match and stood back. Meanwhile, Delta faced a massive operational meltdown after a failed antivirus update led to a global "blue screen of death," resulting in widespread flight cancellations and stranded passengers. In both cases, what made the crisis worse wasn't just the failure itself; it was the scramble, the confusion, and the lack of readiness.

Red teaming for reputation means rehearsing those moments before they happen. It means sitting down with your comms, legal, and HR teams and saying, "Okay, what if someone leaked that Slack thread?" or "What if this old tweet resurfaces during Pride Month?" or "What if a whistleblower goes public tomorrow?"

It's about identifying your blind spots—not just operationally but socially and culturally.

And here's the thing: The threats are no longer slow. They're immediate. Reputation doesn't erode gently anymore; it collapses in real time. Which is why red teaming can't just be a one-off. It has to be a practice. A mindset. A muscle you build so you can react faster, smarter, and with more coherence when the pressure hits.

Some of the best red-team tactics for reputation aren't even that complicated:

- Run *mock crisis simulations* in which your team has to respond to a manufactured but plausible social media firestorm.
- Review your *team's online footprint*. If a journalist or troll went digging, what would they find?
- Draft *reversal narratives*. How would you explain a sudden change in values or policy without sounding hypocritical?
- Test how your internal systems handle a *communication leak*. Who finds out first? Who owns the message? Who panics?

So why don't more companies do this?

Because it's uncomfortable. It takes precious time and attention. It forces leaders to face scenarios they'd rather not imagine. It challenges assumptions and exposes gaps in strategy. It can even ruffle egos. But that discomfort is where the growth happens. The cost of *not* preparing is far greater.

Red-teaming exercises will also force you to focus more diligently on solving data integration issues. Red teaming gives you a chance to spot and repair weaknesses in your reputation strategy, before the proverbial you-know-what hits the fan.

To be clear, this isn't about trying to win a war of public opinion every time. Sometimes, even with the best prep, you'll take a hit. But you'll survive it. And you'll learn from it. That's the difference between a brand with reputational gravity and one that floats wherever the outrage takes it.

So if you haven't already, it might be time to ask: Who on your team is thinking like your enemy? Who is stress-testing your story? Who is preparing for the version of reality where social media turns on you? And by the way, it's probably a good idea to connect with the speak-up culture that already exists in your organization. Employees who challenge the status quo and push back with constructive criticism are not your enemies; they can be your most passionate allies!

Decades in this business have taught me that if you want to survive your worst possible day, you need to rehearse for it and prepare for it before it actually happens.

That's why it makes sense to include red-teaming exercises in your reputation strategy. It's not just about being paranoid or playing devil's advocate. It's about preparing your people for chaos. It's about building muscle memory, understanding and stress-testing your values, and seeing what breaks before the world does it for you.

Companies, like military units, operate in environments of uncertainty and misinformation. The speed of attack, whether it's a missile strike or a viral scandal, leaves no time to build a defense midair. You either anticipated it or you didn't.

But here's what else the military has to teach us: integration. In modern warfare, data flows from satellites to ground units to commanders in near real time. Coordination across domains is essential. Reputation risk requires the same: seamless communication between legal, comms, HR, cybersecurity, and leadership. If your data is fragmented, if insights about internal culture, customer sentiment, or digital vulnerabilities live in silos, then you'll miss the signals that precede reputational collapse.

The future of reputation management isn't just about stronger messages. It's about smarter systems. Red teaming reveals the cracks—but only an integrated data infrastructure can fix them.

TAKEAWAYS

- *Establish* crisis protocols that put reputation at the center of response.
- *Rehearse* scenarios with leadership teams—speed depends on preparation.
- *Document* your reputational assets and deploy them as proof points when tested.
- *Maintain* disciplined messaging; resist the temptation to speculate or overpromise.
- *Recognize* that consistency under pressure preserves long-term equity.

NOTES

Chapter 1

1. PowerReviews, "Survey: The Ever-Growing Power of Reviews," 2023, https://www.powerreviews.com/power-of-reviews-2023/.

Chapter 4

1. Guillermo Arenas, "The Day Michael Jordan's Mother Changed Nike's History Forever: 'Even If You Don't Like It, You're Going to Listen to Them,'" *El País*, April 6, 2023, https://english.elpais.com/culture/2023-04-07/the-day-michael-jordans-mother-changed-nikes-history-forever-even-if-you-dont-like-it-youre-going-to-listen-to-them.html.
2. Casey B. Renner, "Nike Expected $3 Million in Sales—Air Jordan Made $126 Million," *Yahoo! Finance*, July 8, 2025, https://finance.yahoo.com/news/nike-expected-3-million-sales-000133313.html.
3. "How Michael Jordan Revolutionized the Sneaker Industry—and Our Relationship with Shoes," *Temple Now*, April 3, 2023, https://news.temple.edu/news/2023-04-03/how-michael-jordan-revolutionized-sneaker-industry-and-our-relationship-shoes.
4. "'KPop Demon Hunters' Soundtrack Shatters Records as 'Golden' Tops Billboard Global 200," *Associated Press*, January 14, 2025, https://apnews.com/article/b1f1a0390c303fb46959f6cf6e77b5ff; Nick Romano, "2 Fictional K-Pop Groups Are Giving BTS a Run for Their Money," *Entertainment Weekly*, July 1, 2025, https://ew.com/kpop-demon-hunters-soundtrack-huntr-x-saja-boys-give-bts-run-for-their-money-11763738.

5. Veronika, Štičková, "Central Bohemia Comes to Life Again with *Kingdom Come: Deliverance II*," Středočeská Centrála Cestovního Ruchu, July 2, 2025, https://www.sccr.cz/en/central-bohemia-comes-to-life-again-with-kingdom-come-deliverance-ii/; Kristýna Pirková, "Trosky Castle and the Surrounding Area Are Already Feeling the Onslaught of *Kingdom Come* Fans," CT24, April 26, 2025, https://ct24.ceskatelevize.cz/clanek/regiony/hrad-trosky-a-okoli-uz-pocituji-napor-fanousku-hry-kingdom-come-360405; CTK, "New Portal Attracts *Kingdom Come* Fans to Kutná Hora and Bohemian Paradise," CT24, March 7, 2025, https://ct24.ceskatelevize.cz/clanek/kultura/novy-portal-laka-fanousky-kingdom-come-na-kutnohorsko-i-do-ceskeho-raje-358793.

Chapter 6

1. Jamie Whitehead, "Astronomer's 'Clever' PR Move Embracing CEO Scandal Featuring Gwyneth Paltrow," *BBC News*, July 27, 2025, https://www.bbc.com/news/articles/crlzrjp2e2lo; Alisha Gupta, "Gwyneth Paltrow Helps Turn Astronomer's Infamy on Its Head," *New York Times*, July 28, 2025, https://www.nytimes.com/2025/07/28/style/gwyneth-paltrow-astronomer-spokesperson-coldplay-scandal.html.

Chapter 9

1. Robert G. Eccles, Scott C. Newquist, and Roland Schatz, "Reputation and Its Risks," *Harvard Business Review*, February 2007, https://hbr.org/2007/02/reputation-and-its-risks.

Chapter 10

1. Al Root, "Tesla Stock Fell: Why Its Five-Day Winning Streak Ended," *Barron's*, April 8, 2025, https://www.marketwatch.com/articles/tesla-stock-price-trump-tariffs-deliveries-b3879d4f.

2. Chas Danner, "Tesla Is Burning: All the Bad News for Elon Musk's EV Company," *New York Magazine*, March 25, 2025, https://nymag.com/intelligencer/article/latest-bad-tesla-news-elon-musk-stock-price-doge-trump-protests.html.

Chapter 11

1. Stephen G. Adubato, "In Praise of Code-Switching," *Liberal Patriot*, July 22, 2024, https://www.liberalpatriot.com/p/in-praise-of-code-switching.

2. Brittaney Kiefer, "Ikea Slides into DMs with a Cheeky Offer for Late-Night Scrollers," *Adweek*, February 21, 2025, https://www.adweek.com/creativity/ikea-slides-into-dms-with-a-cheeky-offer-for-late-night-scrollers/; Samanta Gladkauskaite, "IKEA to Give Away Free Chips in Brighton This Weekend," *The Argus*, August 9, 2025, https://www.theargus.co.uk/news/25374574.ikea-give-away-free-chips-brighton-weekend/; "Blåhaj," Wikipedia, August 4, 2025, https://en.wikipedia.org/wiki/Bl%C3%A5haj.

Chapter 14

1. "A Deep Dive into the Marketing Strategies of Old Spice," *Brand Hopper,* May 12, 2025, https://thebrandhopper.com/2025/05/12/a-deep-dive-into-the-marketing-strategies-of-old-spice/; Jonathan Calix, "Great Work: An Old Spice Campaign," Abovo Marketing, February 13, 2025, https://www.teamabovo.com/resources/great-work-an-old-spice-campaign/; Narula, Shruti, "Case Study on Successful Viral Marketing of Old Spice," *Digital Vidya*, August 17, 2019, https://www.digitalvidya.com/blog/case-study-on-successful-viral-marketing-of-oldspice/.

2. Rick Rubin, *The Creative Act: A Way of Being* (Penguin Press, 2023), 5–6.

Chapter 18

1. Jean-Marie Dru, *Beyond Disruption: Changing the Rules in the Marketplace* (Wiley, 2002).

2. "Are We Deluding Ourselves About Disruption?" *Media Leader*, July 11, 2022, https://uk.themedialeader.com/are-we-deluding-ourselves-about-disruption/.

3. Barr Balamuth, "Is It Cool to Care Again? What the Embrace of Superman's Sincerity Reveals About Our Cultural Mood," *Sociology of Business*, July 31, 2025, https://andjelicaaa.substack.com/p/is-it-cool-to-care-again.

4. Zoe Ogilvie, "With AI at My Fingertips, Why Do I Need to Use a PR Agency?" *The Times*, January 8, 2025, https://www.thetimes.com/article/238e15e3-30b1-45a2-891e-66e48ff5f891.

Chapter 20

1. Jonathan Scott Morgan, Iman Barjasteh, Cliff Lampe, and Hayder Radha, "The Entropy of Attention and Popularity in YouTube Videos," *arXiv*, December 3, 2014, https://arxiv.org/abs/1412.1185.

2. It's important to remember that consumers who grew up using social media may not bother to send an email to a company or search for a customer service phone when they experience a problem. Instead, they will tag it in a comment or in a story reel and expect a response, whether it's X, Instagram, TikTok, Facebook, LinkedIn, WhatsApp, or other, regardless of whether the company is officially on the specific media. Fast, personalized customer service is now expected directly in the same apps we use to text our family and friends.

3. Ted Gioia, "What Happened to the Celebrities?" *Honest Broker*, March 30, 2025, https://www.honest-broker.com/p/what-happened-to-the-celebrities.

4. Daniel Parris, "How Long Does Music Stardom Last? A Statistical Analysis," *Stat Significant*, August 7, 2024, https://www.statsignificant.com/p/how-long-does-music-stardom-last.

5. Abby Roth, "Do Female Pop Stars Have a Shelf Life?" *Classically Abby*, February 18, 2024, https://www.classicallyabby.com /commentary-lifestyle/do-female-pop-stars-have-a-shelf-life.

6. Kayla Gleason, "Microtrend to Fast Fashion Pipeline," *A Magazine*, September 29, 2024, https://theamag.com/9909/culture/microtrend -to-fast-fashion-pipeline/

7. Eliana Freelund, "Microtrends Have a Macro Impact," *McGill Daily*, February 6, 2023, https://www.mcgilldaily.com/2023/02 /microtrends-have-a-macro-impact/.

Chapter 21

1. Jeanine Moss, "Branding in the Age of Algorithms: Why Algorithmic Fluency Is the New Brand Superpower," Outfront Solutions, https:// www.outfront.solutions/insights/branding-age-algorithms.

2. Moss, "Branding in the Age of Algorithms."

3. Moss, "Branding in the Age of Algorithms."

4. Moss, "Branding in the Age of Algorithms."

Chapter 22

1. Dan Williams, "Strategic Paranoia: When Irrational Fears Serve Rational Ends," *Conspicuous Cognition*, November 23, 2024, https:// www.conspicuouscognition.com/p/strategic-paranoia-when -irrational. See also Thomas C. Schelling, *The Strategy of Conflict* (Harvard University Press, 1980).

2. Williams, "Strategic Paranoia."

3. Keith Dear, Kevin Dutton, and Elaine Fox, "Do 'Watching Eyes' Influence Antisocial Behavior? A Systematic Review and Meta-Analysis," *Evolution and Human Behavior* 40, no. 3 (2019), https:// doi.org/10.1016/j.evolhumbehav.2019.01.006.

4. Dan Williams, "People Embrace Beliefs That Signal Their Traits and Loyalties," *Conspicuous Cognition*, April 6, 2025, https://www.conspicuouscognition.com/p/people-embrace-beliefs-that-signal-354.

5. "*Mutual Aid: A Factor of Evolution*," Wikipedia, April 22, 2026, https://en.wikipedia.org/wiki/Mutual_Aid:_A_Factor_of_Evolution.

6. Matt Ridley, *The Origins of Virtue: Human Instincts and the Evolution of Cooperation* (Viking, 1996).

7. Richard Dawkins, *The Selfish Gene* (Oxford, 1976).

Chapter 25

1. Micha Narberhaus, "A Protopian View of the Emerging Postliberal Era," *Protopia Conversations*, April 8, 2025, https://michanarberhaus.substack.com/p/a-protopian-view-of-the-emerging.

2. "What Exactly Is 'Artificial Inflation of Reputation,' and Where Is the Line?" Stack Overflow, accessed May 5, 2026, https://meta.stackoverflow.com/questions/318497/what-exactly-is-artificial-inflation-of-reputation-and-where-is-the-line; Gurdeep Singh Ransi, "A Hybrid Artificial Reputation Model," *Electronic Theses and Dissertations*, no. 5012 (2014), https://scholar.uwindsor.ca/etd/5012.

3. Wil Wheaton, "Regarding Anonymous Gaming Trolls, Tabletop, and More," *Wil Wheaton Dot Net*, November 11, 2014, https://wilwheaton.net/2014/11/regarding-anonymous-gaming-trolls-tabletop-and-more/.

Chapter 26

1. Alexandra Del Rosario, "'Arcane' Showrunner Calls Netflix Series a 'Love Letter' to 'League of Legends' IP and Gamers; Riot Boss Shares Gaming Company's Next Steps," *Deadline*, November 6, 2021,

https://deadline.com/2021/11/arcane-showrunner-calls-netflix-series-a-love-letter-to-league-of-legends-ip-riot-boss-shares-gaming-companys-next-steps-1234864497/; Television Academy, "Nominees and Winners: 2022—74th Emmy Awards," 2022, https://www.emmys.com/awards/nominees-winners/2022/outstanding-animated-program.

2. Xander Torres, "Why 'Arcane' Has Become a Catalyst for a New Age of League of Legends Fandom," *Nerd Street*, December 17, 2021, https://nerdstreet.com/news/2021/12/arcane-netflix-catalyst-for-league-of-legends-fandom.

3. Y. Mula-Márquez, Begoña Nava-Arquillo, and J. A. Matías-García, "Parasocial Relationships and Identification with Fictional Characters in Adolescents and Adults: A Systematic Review," *Research Square*, March 26, 2024, https://doi.org/10.21203/rs.3.rs-4154497/v1; Melanie C. Green and Markus Appel, "Narrative Transportation: How Stories Shape How We See Ourselves and the World," in *Advances in Experimental Social Psychology*, vol. 70 (Academic Press, 2024), 1–82, https://doi.org/10.1016/bs.aesp.2024.03.002.

4. Katherine N. Lemon and Peter C. Verhoef, "Understanding Customer Experience Throughout the Customer Journey," *Journal of Marketing* 80, no. 6 (2016): 69–96.

5. Robert V. Kozinets, *Netnography: The Essential Guide to Qualitative Social Media Research*, 3rd ed. (Sage, 2019); Ryan M. Milner, *The World Made Meme: Public Conversations and Participatory Media* (MIT Press, 2016).

6. Nestlé Japan, "KitKat History," accessed May 5, 2026, https://kitkat.nestle.jp/history; Nestlé Japan, "KitKat Gift," accessed May 7, 2026, https://kitkat.nestle.jp/gift#shop.

7. Ray Fisman and Tim Sullivan, *The Inner Lives of Markets: How People Shape Them—and They Shape Us* (PublicAffairs, 2016).

Chapter 27

1. Tiffany Regaudie, "Brands Are Mocking Themselves and It Might Be Working," *Banknotes*, February 2, 2022, https://hashtagpaid.com/banknotes/brands-are-mocking-themselves-and-it-might-be-working.

ABOUT THE AUTHOR

CHRIS FOSTER is the CEO of Omnicom Public Relations (OPR), the world's most comprehensive communications network, uniting leading PR, public affairs and policy, and specialty consulting firms across six continents. With deep experience advising Fortune 500 companies and governments across healthcare, energy, finance, and technology, he is known for transforming complexity into clarity—and for helping organizations lead through change.

His first book, *Reputation Strategy and Analytics in a Hyper-Connected World*, details his experiences guiding high-stakes campaigns for governments and global enterprises in defense, healthcare, energy, and technology.